THE LAST OF SEVEN

The Last of Seven

Reflections on a Life in Art

by a former President of the Royal Watercolour Society

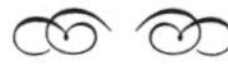

ERNEST GREENWOOD
ARCA PPRWS

BRUSHINGS FARM HOUSE PUBLICATIONS
Ashford

First published 2006

Published by Brushings Farm House Publications
35 Lakeside Place, Chapel Road, Hothfield
Ashford, Kent TN25 4LN.

Book design and production for the publisher by
Bookprint Creative Services, P.O. Box 827, BN21 3YJ, England.
Printed in Great Britain.

Dedicated to

Marion and Kenneth Swan OBE

CONTENTS

ACKNOWLEDGEMENTS

My thanks are due to Frank Burniston, who so willingly transported my work to London exhibitions and also to Fionagh Green, who has a collection of my drawings and paintings. Thank you also to Sir Peter and Lady Wright, and Edward and Diana Wharton Tigar. I am furthermore grateful to Mr Tony Walker and his daughter Wendy without whose early introductions these memoirs would never have been written. But, my grateful thanks go particularly to Emma Willmore, without whose professionalism, advice and patience this work could never have been published.

PREFACE

The following notes and personal observations in these memoirs result from looking back eighty-five years to the fundamental changes that have completely altered the lives and habits of the people in these islands.

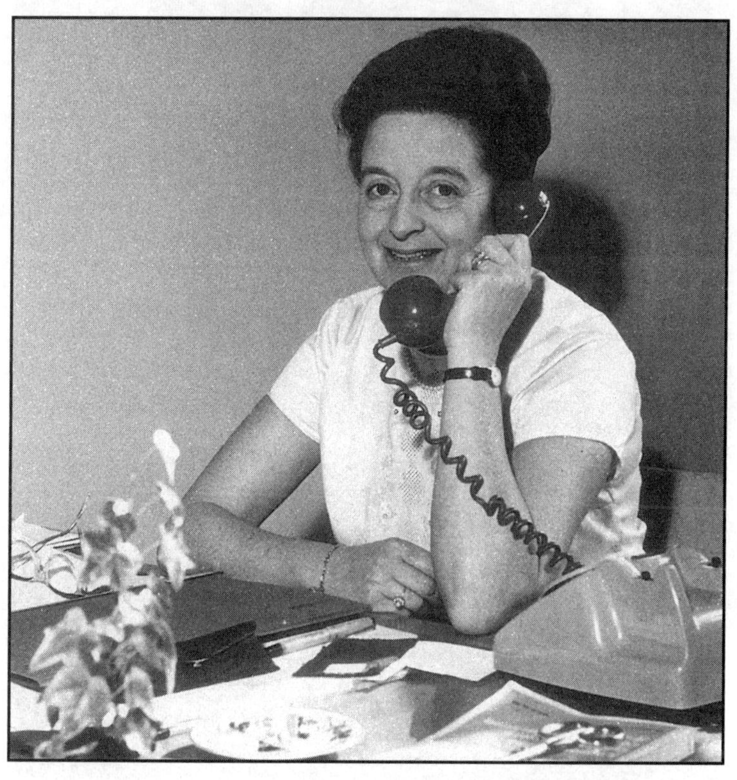

To my wife Eileen, whose unique and varied achievements are mirrored in the following chapters.

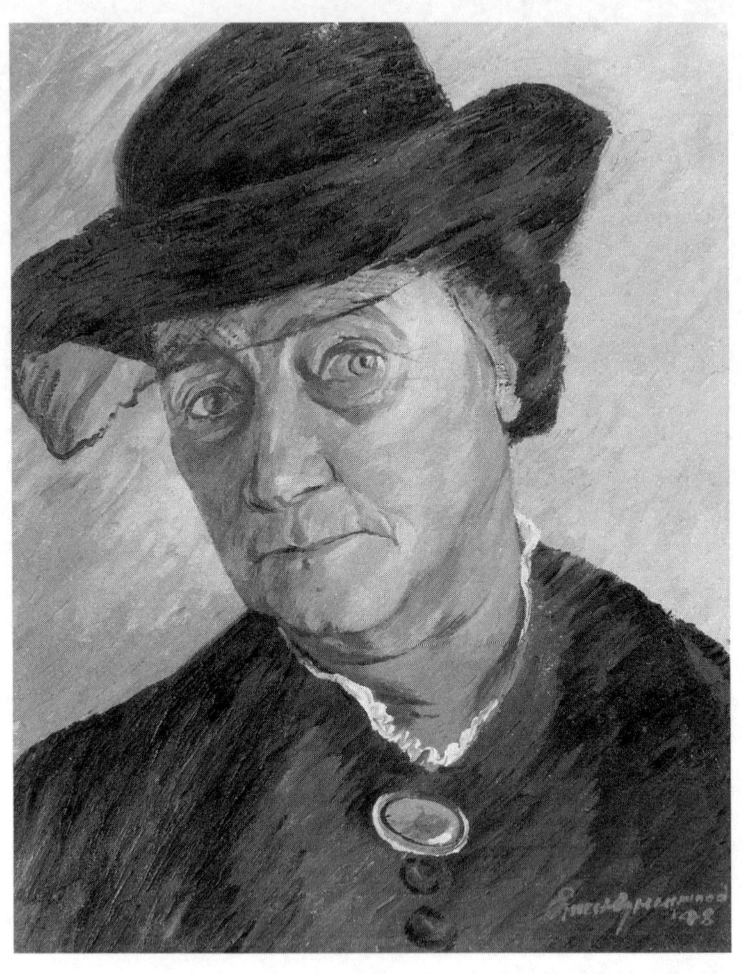

To my mother for her devoted and unselfish support.
She alone made my life in art possible.

I
THE EARLY YEARS

The virtue of parents is a great dowry
Horace, *The Odes*

IF, AS I BELIEVE, the child's education begins before birth, then standards in moral, social and religious conviction ought to exist in the parents at the time of conception. This is a crucial time when the seeds are sown from which the sensibilities develop that make or mar the teenage years, and beyond, into adult life.

The official recognition of 'partners' as a substitute for marriage has seen a considerable retrogression in public morality. The ambiguous phrase 'sex equality', whatever that means, has produced unexpected marital problems in the decline of personal responsibility. Home life with security is all too often being sacrificed for an ephemeral, sexual infatuation which is helping to increase, if not to stimulate, child abuse and cruelty. The popularity of the TV programme Wife Swapping is part of this trend. Juvenile crime and contempt for all authority inside and outside of school continues as we protract form imposing any form of discipline, expecting a government to tell us what to do, and how to act! It would appear that one of the great benefits of 'faith' is the discipline it imposes on the faithful. This is apparent in the pilgrim journeys made by Catholics to Rome, or to Mecca, by thousands who make long, sometimes expensive and difficult journeys to worship at a national shrine. Can you imagine such a pilgrimage ever being made by Anglicans to worship at the shrine of St. Thomas at Canterbury? Just think of the response to such a question! The looks of incredulousness, the cynical half smile . . . The main problem would be cars of course!

The unity and harmony of a good home provides an ideal opportunity for children to be taught the principles of Christian behaviour, better than anywhere else. This is where education originally began. If there is no affection or respect for parents, there will be little for anyone else. What we learn from our parents before the age of five years is all-important. After this age, outside influences begin to assert themselves, or are transmitted directly. Eileen recently made a call by mistake, a wrong number, the phone was answered by a juvenile, under ten by the sounds of the voice, which said, 'Wrong number. Don't do it again – we're pissed off with it'. It was the father speaking through the child, of course.

In spite of these critical comments, I am fully aware of the reverse situation in many lovely homes, but it remains an unfortunate fact that thousands of teenage fans are exhibiting appalling lack of concern for anything, or anybody including their own country. The media are doing nothing to help, by giving so much publicity to all expressions of mass hysteria in the name of sport.

I was six or seven years old when I made a birthday card for my mother which contained features characteristic of work in subsequent years. The picture contained a sailing boat, water

My father Owen Charles Greenwood

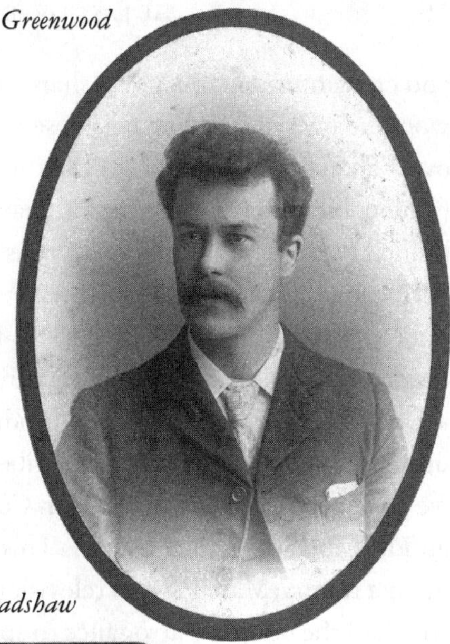

My mother Annie Mildred, née Bradshaw

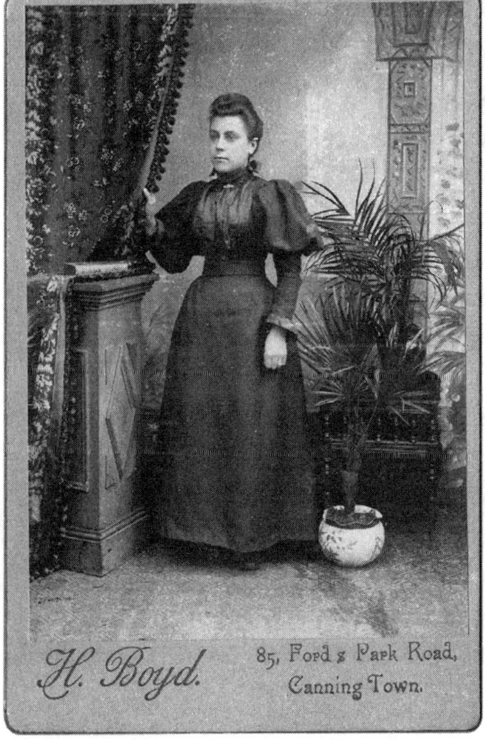

and crescent moon in an oval shape. I have, from time to time, wondered why I should have chosen this particular format – an oval. Then I remembered. At the turn of the last century it was fashionable to have a decoration made by cutting through the branch of a tree on a diagonal, thus producing an oval shape with a flat surface and a bark frame. Upon this, one glued a photograph of Bournemouth, or St. Ives, and used it as a wall decoration. This early form of picture making must have been at the back of my mind when producing Mother's card. My upbringing was, in the best sense, liberal. As with little children we were taught to live by the Ten Commandments, at least as an ideal towards which to aim. This is the place to comment upon a recent (March 2005) television programme by the BBC who had the offensive arrogance to sponsor a team of experts to discuss the relevance of the Ten Commandments today. It was very significant and quite revealing to hear an introduction consisting of the reading of the Ten Commandments, as the reader said, 'to remind you what they are'! I suspect for many it was the first time they had ever been heard in the home or in school. The Ten Commandments were not formulated by a committee of social workers or a conclave of politicians, who are good at making changes. These guides for a better form of living were for people very much like our own (minus the technology), were spoken by a man with a vision who could see clearly the mal-administration, the vice and self indulgence which only has one end. People dislike being reminded of their fundamental short comings. It was with this truth in mind that the Commandments and Beatitudes were addressed to the populace which remained sacrosanct for two thousand five hundred years. Nothing has ever been good enough to last so long. When I was a child courtesy was very important. I was told it was polite to walk on the outside of the pavement, my

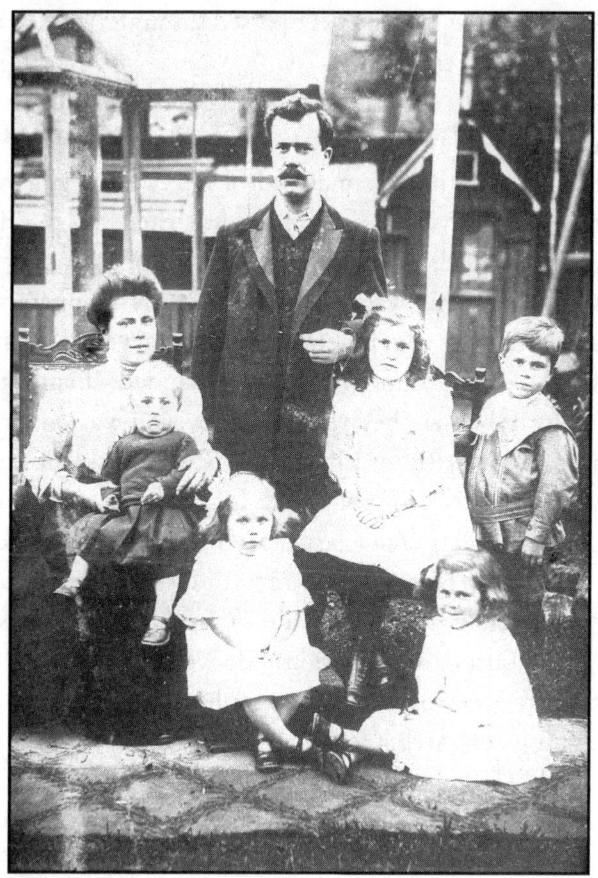

My father and mother and family before I, or my sister were born

sister on the inside. Bad language was never heard. Television had not been born to disseminate the vulgar and often crude humour so entertaining to a large number, which, unfortunately, is caught on so rapidly by the young. Even then, I liked to read, Scott, Hardy, George Eliot, the Brontës. These were the books which I found absorbing and which formed a beginning for further study later on. Although my health was generally good, there were times when I suffered from frequent headaches and nose bleeding, but as I passed through teen age they both stopped worrying me.

Meal time was an important occasion, especially on Saturday and Sunday. No one left the table until everyone had finished eating. When a small child I never enjoyed a sweet until the first course was eaten – until then, no pudding. There was no hardship in this, no compulsion, as this had always been so. This was a time when table manners were inculcated. Recent advertisements showing youngsters sitting on a settee munching a two-handed 'hamburger' followed by a 'bar' as they watched television was unknown. But the very worst thing I have seen was an incident on *Tell the family* in which a number of children compete with each other on the amount of one large cream sponge they could eat in a given time. The result was revolting to watch – animals eat in a less crude manner. As a friend remarked, this is the BBC's contribution to education! I do wonder why the Prime Minister arranged to be seen buying his fish and chips, how far can you go to catch a few votes.

As a child I learned, with a sudden realisation, that life held many sad events, as well as happy ones. It was a warm sunny day. I was out with my mother, when, looking up into the sky, following those of the group around me, I saw the most horrifying sight, that of a huge Zeppelin ablaze, lighting up the sky. Even at that early age the tragedy of such human suffering inside that airship has never left me. Being out with my mother at the time may have contributed to the special relationship I had with her. From the little I knew of Mother's early life, I rather gathered she might have had a sympathy for the Baptists although there was no indication of this until she and I attended a complete immersion ceremony. This took place in a small Baptist Chapel in Crayford. This was my first and last visit and, on reflection, I could not see the relevance in the ceremony with any incident in the New Testament, with which I was familiar. Mother was not a great talker; I can only remember one incident when I heard her express her inner, private feelings which happened when we were moving into Windsor Drive. A wardrobe father had made for her – a special remnant of the past – was being sold for something new and up to date. She and I were at the top of the stairs as the wardrobe was carried down. I heard her say in a soft voice, 'Oh dear, it looks like father's coffin'. Her sad past must have flown by with all its poignancy at that moment, which I have never forgotten.

The weekends were the time, the only times, when the shopping was done. The nearest town was Erith, a place without much character which had grown up piecemeal, in a rather haphazard manner. Judging by my recollection, it was a place without any interests for me – apart from just two. Incidentally, there was little or no transport. Walking the four or five miles to shop was the only way to go, carrying your shopping home afterwards. This was the only way of moving about. If you did not walk, then you stayed where you were! How well I know that now! You walked everywhere. It was no hardship, I walked over four miles to school each day and thought nothing of it. We all walked. To return to Erith . . . weekend shopping on Saturday afternoons was the time to obtain reduced prices on many things. There were no fridges in which to store perishable produce. What was not sold on Saturday went bad and was thrown away.

While mother was engaged on important negotiations over food, I went off to a bookshop, anxious to see if the book for which I craved was still there. For several weeks it still decorated the shop window, then one week it had gone, to my intense disappointment.

The second great interest, always took place in the evening, or late afternoons when the stall holders lit their flares and lamps to illuminate their separate commodities, for all the owners were 'tradesmen', usually only concerned with one aspect of commerce. The supermarket had not yet been imported from America to destroy this aspect of town and country life, which had thrived in England for centuries. The illuminated market held a particular fascination for me. The varied and luminous flares and lamps cast great shadows over humanity, unifying colours and shapes, generating movement and a certain excitement of a dramatic nature, providing excellent material for painters and illustrators.

This was the time that my bicycle years produced some more events. Some miles amongst arable and fruit farmland – now covered with houses and shops – there were, for many years, large fruit orchards from which you could buy quantities of Kentish apples for a few pence a bushel – enough to fill the haversack I carried on my back. On one of these jaunts I was offered and bought some raspberries but I made the mistake of putting the soft fruits in a bag with the apples, with the inevitable result. For on reaching home I was faced with a nasty, red squashy mess. It took much time and effort to get the sack clean again. The Kentish apples I took home bore no resemblance to the graded and highly polished examples one is forced to buy in the supermarkets today. There has been nothing to equal the flavour and quality of those freshly picked apples in my experience since those early days.

But the bicycle – the purchase of a bicycle took some time to realise. My two brothers had bicycles and if I was to get around with them I needed one too. So, in order to find the money to buy one I did all sorts of menial jobs, like chopping wood and cutting grass with hand shears (no mowers!). After some months, through the winter, I saved every penny until I had collected fifteen shillings (old money of course). There is no equivalent sum now, since the change took place, from having 240 pence to a pound, we now have only 100 pence to the pound! This vast sum enabled me to purchase a second hand Raleigh. As indicated, this money was saved in pennies, or six-penny pieces if lucky, over a long period of time. And in the end, the bicycle was not very reliable. It had a fixed driving wheel which tended to be thrown out of alignment with the connecting chain and the back wheel sprocket. This often caused skidding, especially when going down hill, and on one or two occasions almost proved fatal. Fortunately, 'main roads', as they were then called, carried little traffic that was not horse-drawn. It is very different now! One of these bicycle rides, and the longest I can remember, was to Colchester.

Very little contact was made with some relatives, but with one happy exception, which was Aunt May. This could have been because she shared with my Mother a past experience – a major family problem. Uncle Alf was a jolly happy-go-lucky man who once had a flourishing pig business with all the concomitant luxuries, which included a large house and a yacht. However, we knew nothing of the circumstances that brought swine fever to his farm, but it was bad enough to bring bankruptcy and a move into Little Hawksley in Essex. 'Highlands' was a typical Essex, late-medieval, timber framed farmhouse with great character, and I loved it.

It was about this time in my life, I was about ten or eleven years old, that Mother made contact with Father's sister May, with whom my sister and I spent several school holidays. Aunt May was very kind to us. To begin with, my sister and I did the journey by train to Colchester by ourselves. We must have been taken to London and the rest of the way we did with no fear on our part or anxiety on Mother's. Every confidence existed in the civilised behaviour of everyone. Travelling was safe for two little children, even that distance. It was a journey we did several times during the summer holidays. These were lovely times, which have left unforgettable memories, one of which was harvest time.

Aunt had introduced us (if that is the right expression) to a neighbouring farmer's waggoner. He allowed us to mount with the aid of his ladder, to the top of his wagonload of hay. This half-ripe fodder, the colour of terre verte, smelt sweet as only hay can. As the wagon moved off along the lane the layer upon which we sat swayed rhythmically to the gentle movement of the horses. I remember thinking what wonderful animals, as they truly were. Their blue-black rumps looked a long way down from our high perch, but the smell of these powerful horses, their huge bulk the width of shafts, tapering away to a long thin neck, the smell of leather saddling, the jingling of brass decorations of horse and harness is unforgettable. And, of course, from our seats we had extensive views over the surrounding countryside; the little green shoots of wild flowers were just beginning to show through the stubble of the gathered corn. There was no spray with which to kill them off!

Looking back along the land we could see all the festoons of hay torn from the wagon load by the overgrown hedgerows, soon to be enriched by the nuts and blackberries of autumn later to be gathered by country people armed with basket and crooked stick. There are no adjectives that could possibly begin to convey all the senses contributing towards an all absorbing, enveloping experience of exquisite pleasure. Sad to say, that this joy will never again be a reality for future children. They will probably never hear a countryman's dialect talking with an affectionate voice to his horses, suggesting a complete understanding between the two. The all-too familiar smell of tractor oil and the stink of exhaust fumes will constitute the sum total of their lot, unfortunately.

At the end of supper, after a wonderful day, we were lovingly put to bed. On one such night, I had a most terrifying nightmare, which occurs even now. A black, disembodied spirit of evil haunted me, rattling on the door, keeping me awake. On reflection, I think the knocking noise was due to the tapping on the dormer windowpane of the rosy red apples in the morning breeze as they swayed to and fro from the high branches of the old tree. But all this was rapidly forgotten as we descended the winding attic stairs to a welcome porridge breakfast.

There was a year when Owen, Edgar and I spent a holiday together at 'Highlands' with the express purpose of spending time with our cousins, Alfred and Floss. Floss had a strong feeling for family history and started an investigation into our past which has continued with considerable success, with newly discovered relatives in Colchester about whom there is more to relate.

It was a fine morning when the five of us drove off to spend a day on the River Bures. We arrived after some miles' ride, hired a boat and had a very satisfactory picnic some way up stream. When the time came to leave and the packing up was done, we made for the boat and on arrival began to prepare for departure. The four seniors got in and began to arrange our scattered belongings, leaving me to unfasten the mooring and step aboard. But that was when the trouble started; the weight of the four adults at the stern began to take the boat rapidly into mid-stream leaving my feet on the bank while I tried to arrest the drift by holding on to the mooring rope.

The situation caused intense amusement as they watched me slowly pass from a vertical position to a horizontal one, my feet sliding the while from the bank to the water where I ended! The ride home in soaking wet clothes I did not find funny or comfortable. It was good getting back to that warm kitchen.

It seemed to me that the kitchen door was very wide – lovely in summer but a huge black hole from which to keep away draughts in winter. Close to the cottage there grew an ancient, fully-grown walnut tree. Most of the crop was marketed but a considerable number of nuts found their way into Aunt's pickling jars. Almost shaded by the tree was a duck enclosure, surrounded by a tall wire-netting fence. These creatures I found humorously entertaining in their waddling, quacking way and I wanted to pick them up. I found the best way was to fork over the ground encouraging the birds to come for any tasty morsel I might dig up. All I really wanted was the chance to pick one up just to experience the sensuous delight of feeling their smooth feathered backs in contrast to their sharp, cold little feet. This was one of my early realisations of the importance of the tactile sense in the appreciation of so many aspects of life.

No one loves a bully, especially at home. This tendency often showed itself in a sense of failure or even jealousy, which I discovered in Owen. On one afternoon, he caused a most unpleasant incident in the presence of all the family. A complaint was levelled at my sister Jill and was the first sign of deep inferiority. The atmosphere was electric in its unaccustomed intensity. Mother was wonderful, taking no sides but throwing oil on trouble waters. This, and further aspects of his behaviour reflected an inferiority complex. The chip on his shoulder was displayed most forcibly after the attractive woman he thought he was going to marry had turned him down. He was a most unlovable man whose attitude to life became sour. He became difficult to live with. I think he disapproved of my extended studentship for which Mother supported and, in fact, made possible by unstinted generosity. Owen had an unpredictable temper and aggressiveness, which was a help when he joined the army. I think the life suited him well – he made good progress and I feel he was in his element, maintaining a strict discipline at all times to his Commanding Officer's satisfaction, I am sure. His married life was short and he had one son. Owen died when the boy was a teenager. His wife Eunice quickly remarried. This was a branch of the family with whom we had little in common. Owen was singularly unimaginative. It is sad to recall that there was very little mourning at Owen's funeral. The pall of black smoke from the crematorium seemed symbolic; it was almost a confirmation that his life could not have been a very happy one.

Edgar was *so* different. In many ways Edgar had a sad, unfulfilled life. He deserved much better fortune in business and in his married years. His courtship to a most charming woman from a Welsh village lasted a long time. We all thought too long, but they married just before war started.

Edgar was a conscientious objector so he and Susan took up menial work on a farm in Cambridgeshire. Unknown to either of them, Susan had an insipient chest weakness, which was aggravated by life in the Fens. Tuberculosis developed, which Edgar thought would be helped by the fresh mountain air of the Welsh hills, so she went home, leaving Edgar in the South. Susan's condition did not improve and became progressively more serious so Edgar left Gloucester, where he was working for a silk-screen printing business, and began a journey by car, making for north Wales. The evening was grey, misty and cold and got darker as he motored through hilly country, gradually becoming mountainous. In this inhospitable terrain, the car broke down in a remote area. There was no alternative, but to stay where he was until morning. So, making the best of it, as Edgar would, he settled down for the night. Afterwards he said, 'the most difficult thing that night was the constant dripping, drip, drip, of a nearby waterfall'. This rhythmic sound would have a sinister implication to anyone in such a dramatic situation. He was also thirsty and in need of a drink, and very depressed. It was then that the dreadful thought passed through his mind, 'was I going to be too late?' This premonition was all too true – Susan died before he arrived. Her ashes were cast on the mountainside, where Edgar's were to be strewn some years later by his brother-in-law. I'm sure we all felt most deeply about Edgar's sense of loss and ours as well. The rebound to Elsie, the secretary working in the same business as Edgar, was a mistake, although thoroughly understood. Susan was the only woman Edgar ever loved.

Although religious issues were never discussed, Edgar was a liberal-minded man. A thinker with a wide view of moral and doctrinal matters – Elsie was just the reverse. She was a devoted member of the Church of the 'Closed Brethren', expressing all the narrow and often bigoted attitude of this sect. During an exhibition I had in Bedford, to which Edgar and Elsie were invited to the private view, she remained in a room upstairs as she did not approve of this sort of display. The oration given at her funeral service was unbelievable in its medieval turn of phrase and thought. The speaker said 'their sister who had just departed was now in pure white robes living in heaven'. I cannot remember what Edgar's thoughts were but arriving back to his house, Susan's photograph was again on the mantelshelf, which said everything.

Getting up in the morning was never easy for Edgar. On one occasion, leaving Edgar in bed, our sister Connie left for the railway station to catch the early workman's train. This service was to discharge its full load of workers into Charing Cross terminal by eight. On this particular morning Connie set out to walk the mile and a half to the station, leaving Edgar in bed she thought. But on reaching the platform, there was Edgar, smiling, asking, 'Why had the walk taken her so long?' She rightly guessed that a friend passing in a car had given him a lift!

The weekly routine always finished with a walk to the Weslyan Church in Dartford for the evening service. For these three miles walk we were dressed in our best clothes and set out in a solid rank, all eight of us! Rose, Owen and Connie joined the choir and took part in all the associated activities. One of which was carol singing. One year, in order to reduce the time and fatigue of walking several miles, we hired a pony and cart and set out in high spirits to pick up enthusiasts on the way to out first stop. This proved to be a lucrative novelty which did not last long. The motor car was well on its way towards omnipotence.

Connie was the only member of the family to remain unmarried. She had a sweet nature but lacked the ability to contact and make friends in any way likely to forge a lasting relationship in marriage. As a consequence, she made friends with a spinster with whom she spent most of her uneventful life. When Connie and Winifred were both working in London they lived, for a short time, in a Shinecroft cottage similar to the one we had previously occupied.

During this period Mother had no base. She became peripatetic – moving from one house to another. We managed to fix her up in yet another Shinecroft, but she could not live alone and so moved on to Rose and Ben in Letchworth after spending some weeks with us in Bridge Cottage. Mother's last years could not have been happy ones. She never complained about anything but she must have felt lonely and very sad. Her last days were spent in Baldock with Edgar, about which period I have little information, as Edgar was fully occupied running his own screen-printing business. When I did have a note from him it was to say that Mother was ill so I immediately motored to Baldock. Mother was in bed, perfectly lucid, very interested in some photographs of recent paintings I had taken knowing the support she had always given me. Suddenly, looking up, she said 'What do you want Ernest, fame?' This was the last time I saw Mother.

Connie and friend changed jobs and moved away from Otford to the Wirral. On their retirement they bought a bungalow in Barnwell where, after some years, Winnie's memory began to fail and she was moved into an appropriate home. Connie, meanwhile gaining final independence, moved into a charming quadrangle of stone built flats. Here Connie spent her last few days until she died in 2003, a highly respected lady of 91.

I briefly mentioned Jill in connection with the Owen incident in which Jill displayed considerable tolerance. Her calm, unruffled attitude brought about a termination of a most unfortunate outburst in which Jill was viewed in a very favourable light. She and Lilian were both teaching in primary education. Ben had introduced Jill to Sidney – a friend in the RAF. For some years they corresponded until their marriage in the 1940s, which was Jill's goal from the start! In 1961-2 Jill went to Seattle on an exchange basis for one year. During her absence her two children, Graham and Pauline, stayed with us at Brushings Farm House. We have remained in touch with Pauline and were delighted to see her in August 2004. Of Graham we know very little In 1958, Sidney died and Jill took on the headship of a primary school in Northamptonshire where she became friendly with a member of the ancient family of the Brudenalls. She died whilst visiting the hairdresser in 1994, in Kettering.

Sister Rose, being the eldest member of the family, was the one who shared with Mother the various problems which arose and, in consequence, tended to be self-opinionated. She took the stance of being wise and well informed but this became less noticeable as time passed. She was ambitious and kept Ben to the grindstone during his slog to gain a qualification to enable him to become a teacher of craft. When he was appointed to a vacancy in Letchworth they moved into a large Edwardian house where they settled and remained for many years. In many ways Rose had a colourless, rather neutral personality. Her marriage to Ben was never consummated. He turned up one day in great distress and in an oblique way, indicated what had transpired. He had apparently gone in to the bedroom smelling strongly of cigarette smoke, the odour of which Rose could not abide. The unsavoury incident in which Rose had suddenly been completely overcome was probably the result of a lifetime restraint with a man she had never felt passionate towards. Ben worked for Rose most unselfishly – he did everything she wanted, except be a different man. Ben loved, but was never loved, in spite of early courtship indications to the contrary. What a difficult thing marriage is!

Lilian left Dartford Grammar School for Girls and did a teacher training for infants. Lilian and Frank met while on holiday. Lilian called with Frank on his way home, while Edgar and I had got the place in a 'fine pickle' decorating the sitting room. Appropriate apologies were made but the situation had no influence on the outcome. Lilian and Frank got married and she went north to Darlington, Frank's hometown. We paid them a visit once when they were hosts to 'the family bundo'. This was a yearly event with each pair arranging a venue. I think this was Mother's idea as a means of keeping the family intact. This organisation was augmented by the family journal, which was posted to each in turn once the individual contribution had been written. If these journals have survived, they should make for interesting reading for future generations.

It was on one of these 'bundo' visits that I experienced the long and tedious drive to Scotch Corner and beyond to Darlington where we paused before going on to our luncheon. The house Lilian and Frank lived in with their daughter Julia was suburban in every way as were their lives and interests – dull and uneventful. Lilian made several efforts to maintain her piano playing but after considerable discouragement and criticism from Frank she gave up except for the church, which seemed to be their main, narrow interest.

As far as I can recall, they seldom, if ever, had a real holiday, never went abroad, or extended their lives much beyond Darlington. Frank was no driver; after two or three car accidents in which they both suffered injuries Lilian refused to be driven by him anymore. She brought her own little car and ran it out of her modest income with no help from Frank. Such were their fragile relationships. Their son, Martin, revealed a flair for humorous speaking which was quite entertaining. He kept everyone amused during the wedding ceremony when he married Nester. He continues to be loquacious in the annual letter he writes to us at Christmas from Edmonton. They have made their home in Canada, where their children were born. Martin came home to attend his parents' funerals. He had no time to travel south to see us, but did send a note of regrets.

This survey of the family shows a group of related people with entirely diverse and contrasting temperaments, with little interest in each other's need or ambitions. At least, they were seldom expressed and less so as they grew older, made their own friends, and married. Lilian's death, partially due to the car accidents she suffered, brought to an end a life that had very few great moments, very few outstanding events to add a little colour to her life in Darlington.

II

ART EDUCATION: GRAVESEND SCHOOL OF ART

As already indicated, Mother was my champion. Ever since my special twelfth birthday and gift she understood that I only wanted to study art. To achieve the means whereby I might be able to do this she went to endless trouble, eventually seeking an interview with the local Education Officer. The outcome was hopeful. I had a meeting with the Headmaster of Gravesend School of Art. I was admitted into the junior department. My travelling expenses were for the train journey from Dartford to Gravesend only. The distance from home to the station was a good twenty minutes walk. It seemed longer at night after evening classes as I did not get home until after ten o'clock to enjoy supper! I was not long in the junior school when I entered the life class and began to feel my way towards the first rung of the ladder. I shall never forget Mother's face when, at the age of fifteen, I showed her my first life-drawings. I think this event and her reactions (remembering this was in the 1930s) revealed what an effort she made to understand and appreciate something of which she had no previous knowledge. From that day I had her permanent interest and support. I could always talk to her about anything and had a sympathetic ear, but often without comment. I was left to make up my own mind! Needless to say, I was only corrected once. The word I used was 'damn' – that was enough. I respected her too much ever to be offensive again or do anything of which she disapproved.

Life from now onwards changed and I developed rapidly, becoming absorbed into a new world of opportunity. The acceleration began with the arrival of a senior student from Beckenham School of Art. Why he should ever have come to Gravesend from a much more senior and prestigious establishment we never knew. He was considerably older than we were, well read and a splendid draughtsman. He opened my eyes. I saw just how academic and sterile the teaching was, how lazy, self-satisfied and insular the staff were. Many of the students tended to be the same, especially the women who seemed to float in and out of classes aimlessly.

This senior student, Roy Botting, lent me a book on the Renaissance – the first history of the period I had ever read. Strange as it seems now, the school had next to nothing of a library, just a few miscellaneous, tired-looking, shoddy volumes which, to my knowledge, no one read anyway. But this first history did everything for me. I joined the Dartford library, the first book lent to me by Botting was a kind of springboard. One book led me on to the next, the subject matter and vocabulary becoming more demanding, wider and wider. John Crawley gave me *The Two Carlyles* (which I had until recently). Carlyle introduced me to the German philosophers and poets. I read all the plays and writings of Schiller, Goethe, Winkelmann. I read Kant, Nietzsche, Descartes and the French philosopher Comte. I cannot remember much of the substance of my reading, which kept me up to the early hours, but I saw the world of knowledge and art opening up to me with great satisfaction. The revelation of the third and fourth years at the art school was beginning to provide the substance for which I was searching.

I saw Goethe and Schiller in the same mould as Beethoven and Schubert and they in turn to Michelangelo and Raphael whose work I was in the process of discovering. Although, Mr. Miller, the Headmaster, became a real friend and helped in many ways, he disagreed with my deviation from the course, or rather the way I was treating the teaching. He was anxious for me to get a place at the college; so was I, but on my terms. When I come to think about it now, I was very young – sixteen years with no justification for arguing with an experienced practitioner. On one occasion he threatened to terminate my studentship. At the time I was drawing a plaster cast of 'The Boy and the Goose', a Hellenistic work little thought of now. This was one of several life-sized casts of famous sculptures such as the 'Discobolus', 'The Venus de Milos' and the 'Germanicus' now no longer used in contemporary teaching which, like so much of the past, has been discarded. I remember my feelings over this issue. My drawing was firstly, too big and, secondly, much too black, being almost covered by soft lead pencil. The very opposite of what it should have been, but things improved after this hiccup!

The art school days brought together two or three students who, in different degrees, remained friends. Ron Dalzell, full of self-confidence, was a little man with exceptional energy and a sense of humour. But we never knew what prompted him to come to school one morning (and only one) wearing a bowler hat! It made him look like a professional comedian and caused such a sensation that he never lived it down. We became life-long friends and, as he was two or three years my senior, was very helpful on several occasion in spite of our interests and temperaments being so different.

The other members of our small class were John Crawley, a very gifted young man, who died at an early age with tuberculosis. Ron and I went to see him where he was living with his wife (also an ex-art student) in a bungalow near Meopham. He was very ill, but explained that he had ordered a stirrup pump to clear the congestion in his lungs. His ability to make fun and light of a situation he knew to be terminal was typical of a person of great character, as John certainly was. It was in my second year at college when Ron made friends with a sculptor living in Tenterden. The family had a flourishing business in the town to which we were invited during the summer vacation. So Ron, John and I organised the walk from Gravesend to Tenterden spending one night under canvas on the bank of the Medway. The exact route I cannot remember, but I do recall that the night was very cold. We had one blanket each and I suggested we made one bed sharing the three blankets. This proposal was turned down flat, so we suffered a chilly night until, with a rapidly evaporating morning mist, we dived into the river before lighting a fire to cook breakfast. Ron showed very little ability over this simple operation but we managed in the end and walked on to Tenterden. I was wearing a new pair of brown shoes that cost me seven shillings (they were a bit too big for me!) On arrival at Kim's home we were rather reluctantly ushered into the drawing room for what proved to be a very short stay. Much to John's amusement, on departure, we were offered one Victoria plum each before walking back to Gravesend. I had a distinct feeling that we were not approved of by Kim's mother.

Ron and John were two real friends. On my twenty-first birthday they gave me the complete works of Shakespeare which, naturally, I valued, and was sorry to see it go.

Little need be said of Tom Kay, the third member of the class. He had a rather supercilious attitude towards the school. There was little warmth in his character. It kept him aloof as Eileen and I were to discover some years later when, as founder principal of Sittingbourne College, Eileen negotiated an advanced course for some students. Tom was senior inspector in the Ministry of Education, and did we know it!

It is natural that students should experiment with new and traditional techniques, one of which was the use of gesso for making a ground on which to paint in oil or watercolour. This substance was made with whitening and size. Unless used soon after manufacture it went 'off' quickly. During a lesson on perspective given by the headmaster, a certain unfamiliar expression passed over his face, after a short time it deepened into one of disapproval, obviously from a particular smell, but not from a member of the class we hoped! Disapproval soon passed to one of disgust as he and we caught the effluvia of a distinct stink, a strong vintage, emanating from a hidden source which we all paused to investigate. We found it. Hidden behind a screen was a jar of rotten gesso – someone had forgotten it – to our temporary discomfort. Years later we had a second experience of this in Redcliffe Road.

Ron left for the Royal College of Art that September but we remained in contact until his marriage which took place soon after his appointment as art master at Bromley Grammar School for Boys. He married Molly, a past student of Gravesend School of Art. I was so pleased to be asked to be Ron's best man which prompted some amusing comments. Ron seldom looked smart. Whatever he wore never seemed to fit, rather like the American policeman Colombo. By contrast, not knowing what to expect, I went looking as smart as I knew how. I even borrowed a pair of spats from Ben. I must have looked the part, being mistaken for the groom!

In many respects, Ron was an ambitious teacher with a special interest in seventeenth and eighteenth century architecture. For some years he lectured up and down the country for NATFAS eventually receiving an invitation to New York where he was a great success. Strangely enough, Eileen (Meem) and I stayed in the same hostel that Ron had used a year or two later during one of our own ten visits to New York and the USA. The last time I saw Ron was in 1997 when he came to my last exhibition held in Maidstone. In spite of a lifetime friendship Ron only had criticism for the exhibition which was rather disappointing, especially as it proved to be our last meeting. Since then, judging by the information and type of correspondence, I felt Ron was feeling his 93 years. Sadly, Molly died in December 2003, and Ron four days after, so ending a life-long friendship of eighty years.

The following summer I took the entrance examination to the Royal College of Art – but not well enough. This meant another year in Gravesend which the Headmaster made possible by offering me a one year pupil teaching job (now no longer allowed). This was my salvation in many ways. At home the family became restless and resentful of my prolonged studentship. I was now nearly eighteen years old and looking to another three years in Kensington. Mother, of course, was a great help, particularly in the matter of essentials, like clothing. I am sure now that my needs came first even if hers went short, as I think they did. Looking back, I am not sure that I was as appreciative as I should have been. After all, I stayed at the college for another three and a half years.

One thing I do remember clearly during the antique drawing periods was the sudden entry into the room of Mr. Miller (the headmaster) with two female visitors who proved to be the Countess Darnley (late of Cobham Hall) and her daughter, a young, very handsome woman of about twenty years. When she spoke, the most beautiful sounds came from her throat. For me, an impressionable young man, her voice was magic, with a musical sonority – never to be forgotten – but envied. The only voices I have heard to bear any comparison were from Kathleen Ferrier and Lawrence Olivier. It was the music in their speech which made listening compulsive!

In my second entrance examination I must have done well enough because I was summoned by the college registrar to attend an interview with the principal Sir William Rothenstein. I was admitted, but without scholarship support. I cannot remember how it was Mother made friends with the headmistress of a certain secondary modern girls' school. She had a most unusual name. I suppose it was Mother again who must have mentioned my predicament because she called on us one day and handed me ten crisp five pound notes (the type now long forgotten). It was like passing to me £500 with every trust and confidence. She was so generous, taking me for runs in her car and giving me the support I needed. When my unsuccessful decoration for the Prix de Rome was returned to me, a six foot by three foot panel, she had it erected in the hall at her school.

I was admitted but probably gave most inadequate answers to his questions. But I am sure I was not the only one! In one of the monthly criticisms given by Sir William in the Victoria and Albert Museum lecture theatre, he commented on the fact that so few students being interviewed wished to make college a beginning of a life in art. On reflection, the number of students who went on to make international reputations was very small indeed, the exceptional ones being Henry

Moore and John Piper. And so my college days began in 1932, with a silent wish to make some small impact on the art world – which never happened.

III

FURTHER ART EDUCATION

Royal College of Art, Kensington – Italy, 1932.

I HAD A LOT TO LEARN, a long way to go. I was kept in the life-class well into my second year before being allowed into the painting school. I learned very little from the staff as I found the teaching was casual and not very stimulating. We were left to learn from each other, including the growing-up experiences of youth, which we did! I learned a great deal from observing methods of working from senior students. The occasional talks in the V&A lecture theatre were not very good in my opinion, even then. I was happy to go on with my own reading by which time I had dispensed with a brief acquaintance with Christian Science and other faiths, old and new, but in this realm of thinking I was content with the Ten Commandments and the Beatitudes to provide a basis for daily living.

By this time Ron was doing a pedagogy course, having passed his exams. He was now ARCA. For his final year we shared digs in the Fulham Road bed and breakfast which cost us ten shillings a week. This was a large sum out of our £75 annual scholarship money, but we managed with thrift and humour – sometimes misplaced! Ron had a poster to design for some function or other and decided to work on it in the digs using the mouth spray technique. Our Victorian room boasted a marble fire-surround and a large over-mantel mirror. This example of bygone opulence was rather overshadowed by two cheap beds, a kitchen table much worn and two chairs. The remaining space was not large especially for producing a poster, but Ron ploughed on using his mouth spray. All went smoothly until I noticed a few sprays on the mantle shelf. On closer examination, I noticed the mess Ron was making. Not only was the mantle liberally painted in fine spots, but also the mirror and chair backs. Now, for some unknown reason, the situation struck me as being very funny and I began to laugh. Of course, the more I laughed, the more annoyed Ron became until finally, having recovered, I helped him clean up and we resumed our good natured relationship.

My interest in orchestral and chamber music resulted from a complimentary ticket I found in the college common room. From this chance find I became the first self-appointed general secretary of a non-existent music society.

It was very pleasant, especially on warm summer evenings, to walk up Exhibition Road, through Hyde Park and so into Wigmore Street, where there used to be two small concert halls: the Wigmore and the Aeoleon Hall. They were two small halls in which young musicians worked their way up towards the international platform. It was with these small enthusiastic audiences that I enjoyed so much the chamber music which augmented my other work in the college. I always went to these concerts on my own. I went once, and only once, with a girl student from the painting school, but this was to the Queen's Hall (destroyed by bombs during the war) to hear, for the first time, Beethoven's Choral Symphony in which I was pleased to have read Schiller's 'Ode to Joy' (which Beethoven had used during the choral section). It was about this time I had a most pleasant surprise. Allen Sorrell, one of the drawing school tutors, asked me if I would care to assist him in his work on two large panels commissioned by Southend Museum and Art Gallery. I learnt a lot during the work I did for him. We became friends until he moved away and I left college. But he did come to our first little exhibition in Redcliffe Road.

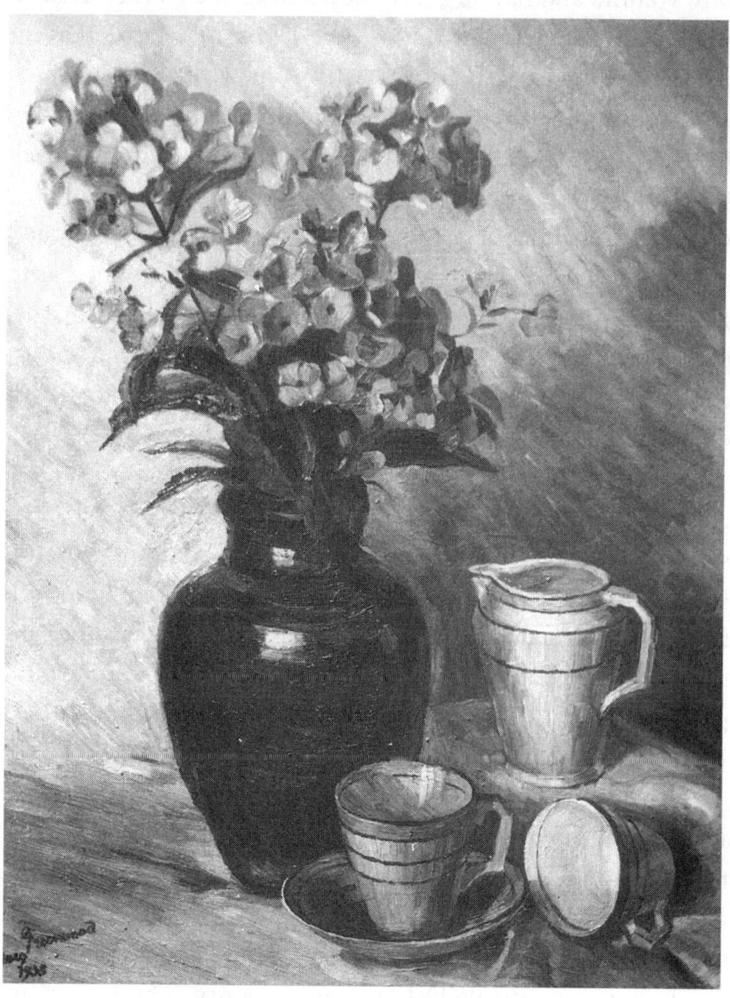

One of the paintings done at this time

Back in the college, one of the exceptional amenities, no longer immediately available to students, now housed in the their own buildings, was the V&A library, and of course, the museum itself, with its inexhaustible treasures of interest and instruction. The little green lights over the reading desks and the soft tread of the ageing library assistants who brought a rare volume and laid it gently down onto the leather desk, I shall always remember. It was here I first met James Laver, curator of drawings and prints, who, some years later, opened an exhibition of our watercolours and Eileen's prints in the Kensington Art Gallery. Here we made friends with Michael Chuse, who later on moved to the Zwemer Gallery in the Charing Cross Road. He and his second wife, Valery Thornton, the well known printmaker, paid a visit to Brushings Farm House. We kept in touch until his death sometime in the turn of the century. Shortly after Michael left for a new post, the entire block of the handsome Edwardian Terraces was demolished.

It was James Laver who suggested I might like to take a class in the Mornington Crescent Working Men's Club. He said this was purely job experience which I could find useful in the future. So I took his suggestion and talked about all sorts of things during drawing lessons with a number of poorly educated, unemployed young men. I had my tube fare paid only, but I did enjoy and find the experience helpful as James Laver said I might.

All this time, war clouds were gathering over Europe. Hitler was rapidly taking the Nazi Party and the German nation into an aggressive, domineering and ambitious policy aiming at the control of Europe by fair or, as history has shown in Hitler's case, foul and foreboding means.

These crept into daily life as uncertainty. The grammar

school routine was broken by whole periods being taken up filling sandbags to protect the main assembly hall. One or two members of the stall had gone either to volunteer or after receiving calling-up papers. Some sixth-form students also found important work before I received mine from His Majesty in the demand for my services! The times brought acceleration to many things which would otherwise have been taken more leisurely. One of these was marriage, but my trip to Rome came first.

I was in my third year in the Royal College and I had work to do on portraiture. I was in need of a sitter. Walking along the women's corridor I stopped a student I had not seen before and asked if she would care to sit for me. A sitting was arranged in the V&A, my only studio, behind one of the screens for a little privacy from passing visitor who were more interested in the unexpected than the particular exhibit they had come to see. In my opinion I did not think much of what I had done. Russell now has the cut-down painting – the head only.

Shortly afterwards I had a letter from my friend Adrian Beech. He was writing from Rome having been awarded the Prix de Rome scholarship for etching and engraving. I never knew why, he being a confirmed painter in oil on canvas. Be that as it may, the letter was a warm invitation for me to join him in Rome at the British School. It was a bit awkward, but inviting. I had just been awarded a continuation scholarship myself. How could I take this monthly allowance when in Rome? I asked the principal, Sir William Rothenstein, who said, 'Yes, Greenwood, you go to Rome'. When I mentioned the monthly scholarship he said, 'ask a friend to collect the cash for you. A college friend would I'm sure, do this'. And so it was arranged and I made tracks for Rome.

Now I had never been abroad before. This was an entirely new and unexpected opportunity. I was young for my age. Edgar came to Victoria station with me. I bought my return ticket to 'Roma Centrali', for £7 equal to about £350 in present day money. I travelled third class all the way which was, for me, the greatest adventure of my life.

The train huffed and puffed its way through France and on to the lower steps of the Alps. I had never seen mountains before. I thought they were wonderful, magnificent. The waterfalls, lucid and glass like in their luminous transparencies were a revelation. The light snow-capped peaks enveloped in the pale turquoise haze of the morning were just magic to me. These new things seen, remained in my memory until the train, drawing into a siding, stopped and the following bustle and shouting suggested that something special was about to take place. The 'something special' was the fact that the train had come to a standstill for the night. Now this was if not alarming then disconcerting. From Victoria I had travelled on hard, wooden-slatted seats. No upholstery, no heating, no buffet, no human comforts at all. How glad I was of the small travelling rug my thoughtful grandmother had given me, knowing I was travelling alone.

* * *

Grandma Bradshaw was a small lady of great natural charm. I can remember so well her small decorated Victorian blue-black bonnet with the hat pins securing it to her hair sticking out at the back, and her soft leather, button-up boots kept warm in the hearth by the all-caring Aunt Eddie. I frequently made the journey by No. 8 bus from college to see her.

Grandpa Bradshaw had died a few years before, so Grandma lived with two unmarried daughters on the upper floors of a typically large Edwardian terraced house. Steps led up to the front door while, through iron railings, a gate gave onto steps going down to the basement, kitchen and scullery; the latter always smelling strongly of carbolic soap. I remember the seldom used gas-lit parlour, as it was called. The spluttering 'pop' as the gas ignited illuminated the parlour with its slightly musty smell. The gas mantle shed a soft blue light over the room. The cast iron fireplace with its surrounding coloured tiles had an over-mantle covered with a lightly faded apple-green runner with a fringe of hanging bobbles. This proudly supported a black marble clock which had on each side a pair of rearing horses, with their energetic, struggling trainers. I wonder what became of this clock, now a collector's item.

I particularly recollect the night visits, the walk from the bus stop and through the small park. These were the days of wet, cold and foggy evenings when, on either side of the gravelled path, the trees shed showers of clammy cold water over your outer garments. Arriving at Grandma's house was like walking into a dimly lit warm cave with a little meal prepared by Aunt Eddie. She was severely handicapped and did not have a long life after Grandma died. She had devoted her life to the welfare of her mother whom she loved. I think, of her grandchildren, I was the favoured one probably because I was named after the son who was killed at the Dardanelles, aged eighteen. He was a particularly gifted young man who, like so many, was fruitlessly sacrificed. When I came of age twenty one, Grandma presented me with his small Bible, which gave the name of the church in which Nanna was married (the church of St. James the Less), together with a message from the vicar. It was my intention to offer, at the appropriate time, this Bible to the third Ernest as a keepsake. How mistaken one can be; the book is gone! Grandma Bradshaw was the complete antithesis of Grandma Greenwood. I was very fond of the former who, on my twenty-first birthday, gave me a pair of gold cufflinks, one of which I regrettably lost in the Cheddar Gorge.

* * *

To return to my journey, there was nothing for it but to do what the other travellers were doing – getting as comfortable as possible under uncongenial circumstances. And so we slept. The morning was bright and cheerful. Everyone got up, stretched, yawned, coughed themselves awake and thought about food. We were all hungry. The train eventually started again and pulled into a platform where, glory be, a young boy was selling filled rolls. We gratefully bought what we could and settled down for a long journey to Rome.

There were not many stops. People got in and out without much notice being given to anyone. The portion of the train I was in contained very few passengers, none of note, until at a more rural station an elderly peasant woman got in with a white nanny goat. She gave me a half smile before settling down to relax in a corner seat. The white goat did its best to follow her good example on the floor. At a few stops down the line they got out. All doors were slammed shut and the train moved on, then I saw that the goat had obligingly left its card behind, with which memento I spent the rest of the journey.

It was mid morning when we arrived at Rome Central. You can imagine my relief to see Adrian's cherub-like, round, pink face looking over the barrier. With the minimal of salutations and questions about the journey we moved off by bus to the British School. I cannot recall a great deal of my life there other than the apartments. These were designed essentially as studios with a balcony and staircase at one end giving access to a room which provided and contained all the necessary amenities for daily life including bed and storage facilities. The communal eating arrangements followed a university pattern. We were served by waiters for meals, except breakfast, which took the form of a buffet. I thought the standard was very good but did not encourage conversation as most of the scholars were pursuing individual lines of study.

Although we spent time working in respective studios, Adrian and I worked in one of the others for life drawing, but most of our time we were out exploring the sites of the ancient city and travelling. The exploration of Rome quite naturally came first. 'The Capital', St. Peters, the Vatican, contained hardly one visitor, enabling us to study some of its many treasures unhindered. The sculptures and frescoes in the Pope's apartments were more impressive than I thought they might be, with the creations of Raphael and Michelangelo being the most powerful. Raphael's 'Parnassus' and 'School of Athens' revealed the extent to which Raphael was familiar with the newly discovered Greek and Roman poets and philosophers who, fundamentally, made possible fifteenth century 'Humanism'. Raphael's achievement was just wonderful, especially when one remembers that so many remarkable artists like Schubert and Mozart died in their early thirties. Raphael died aged thirty-seven from the plague, as did a number of great scholars who made the Renaissance the turning point from medievalism into a period of discovery with logical, systematic thinking into every aspect of technology from Leonardo to travelling thousands of miles into space.

Raphael's astonishing achievement was only made possible by having the assistance of trained, gifted young painters serving an apprenticeship in his workshop. This fact often makes attribution of some works difficult, hence the phrase 'the workshop of'. But indubitably, the Sistine Chapel's vast decorations were as overwhelming as purported by travellers and art historians alike. That so much complicated technical competence together with original creative power could be produced by one man and an assistant in so short a time was beyond comprehension. By this time, Michelangelo was not a young man. The buon fresco method of large-scale wall decoration required considerable physical stamina. Following all the preliminary work of conceiving, designing, and drawing the cartoons, the painter was able to transfer to the damp plaster the painting which stands unique, and which we were privilege to enjoy on our own. The Sacristan unlocked the doors, ushered us in, and handed each of us a two handled mirror with which we were able to see in detail and examine the work in comfort. Our second visit, while on a Swan Hellenic cruise some years later, was an appalling experience. No limit was placed on the number of visitors admitted. We stood shoulder-to-shoulder, unable to see anything, and had there been an emergency one could not have left in safety. Perhaps conditions of entry have improved since the late 1930s. But to return to the chapel. These decorations were quite overwhelming. Every figure on that ceiling had to be drawn full size before being transferred to the curved surface. If only some of those could have survived! The chapel exerted a strong, indefinable influence on us. There was nothing, there was no one to interrupt a deep appreciation for such a unique achievement in painting and architecture. 'The Last

Judgment', sixty foot by forty foot (two hundred and forty square feet) was overpowering, dominating everything on walls or ceiling. The silence, the stillness, also helped to produce a feeling of time held in abeyance. The everlasting influence of great works was a realisation we both experienced in silence and made no attempt to define.

On leaving, and stepping into strong sunlight, we continued to explore the scattered and extensive ruins of the Eternal City. These fragments required considerable imagination and study in order to give these remains of a past great splendour the unified dignity they once had. Raphael was the first ever director of public monuments, appointed to stop the destruction of ancient buildings. Because of many invasions, sacks and pillages, the remnants of the city had been being destroyed by medieval peasants in order to obtain lime for the plastering of their huts and cow sheds. Many avenues and temple columns were raised, many more taken away by subsequent invaders to build Christian churches from precious ready-made materials. Raphael had a major job to do to save what was left.

I have often wondered why so many great men managed to produce so much work. So often during these times life was short; Mozart died in his late twenties, Schubert in his thirties, Raphael in his thirties too. But Raphael, as was common, trained gifted young men serving an apprenticeship to work under the direction of the master in a *Bottega* (a workshop). They often completed unfinished paintings, a process that makes positive identification in a number of cases very difficult and brings about the phrase 'in the workshop of'.

Life in the British School was relaxed in a scholarly atmosphere. We were all very much concerned with out own specialist interests in a leisurely way without creating any feeling of insecurity. The director of the School, Elis Waterhouse, was also the librarian. He was engaged in writing a book on *Baroque and Rococo Painting and Sculpture*, a copy of which once formed part of the *Pelican History of Art* which stopped after about eight publications.

Later on, we planned a visit to Urbino, the Palace of Frederico Montefeltro, and the birthplace of Raphael. We went by train but before setting off, we decided to spend a day in the minute state of San Marino, isolated on its mountain height almost in the centre of Italy, providing extensive panoramic views over miles of verdant countryside into an unpolluted haze. As I had discovered, travelling in the 1930s still had much of the previous centuries primitive character, as was emphasised as we travelled towards Urbino.

This little, walled town had the medieval appearance of an illuminated miniature by one of the Limburgh brothers. It cannot have changed for centuries. No cars, no buses, no wide roads for fast travellers impatient to get somewhere and no petrol stations, but it did have a railway. We arrived in the late afternoon and booked into a small hotel for bed and breakfast then hurried out to make the most of the remaining day. Our first concern was to get into the Palace before sundown. This honey-coloured building, a mixture of Lombardic Gothic and Classical features was built for Frederico Montefeltro. This man made famous by the double portrait of himself and wife in profile by Piero della Francesca reveals a strong determined character with a great hooked nose (closely resembling a beak) above a sensitive mouth. He was a great patron of the arts, a collector and supporter of many artists, including P. della Francesca, whose picture 'The Flagellation' we saw on an easel all by itself in a courtyard of the Palace. There were so few visitors, none of whom would have thought theft was possible from anyone, indicative of the state of morality at the time. Now the infamous worldwide trade in works of art, the prices paid at auctions, the proliferation of television programmes, road shows and boot sales have all helped to put the theft of works of art high on the list of profitable robbery by well-organised gangs. Now the strict security of particularly valuable works of all kinds in our museums has become such an expensive and necessary responsibility.

We returned to our hotel, had some food of sorts and went to bed in readiness for another day of study, remembering our one object was information and appreciation, the original reason for the 'Grand Tour' of the eighteenth and nineteenth centuries. What is activating tourism now, but profits from transport and hotel owners, now money comes first. As you may have guessed, we travelled very lightly. No refinements, just the essentials, just and only 'just'! When we got up in the morning to prepare for our next goal, Adrian, having turned back his sheets said, 'Ernest, these sheets have been used before we slept in them'. Our boarding house might have been a bawdy house for all we knew, or cared. We had the treasures of Arezzo uppermost in our minds. Even so, we only had time for one visit to Saint Apolloniare, just outside Arezzo in Classe. This great church, built in red brick in Lombardic Romanesque contains one of the few remaining great mosaic decorations in Italy which we were delighted to see. I should have kept a diary or notebook. I suppose I was ill prepared for so much to overwhelm me, especially on subsequent visits to Rome where there was no time to pause long before the next site or building occupied out concentrated attention. This Italian period consolidated my interest in the Renaissance, its origins and subsequent influence on European art and architecture. My term at the British School ended all too soon and

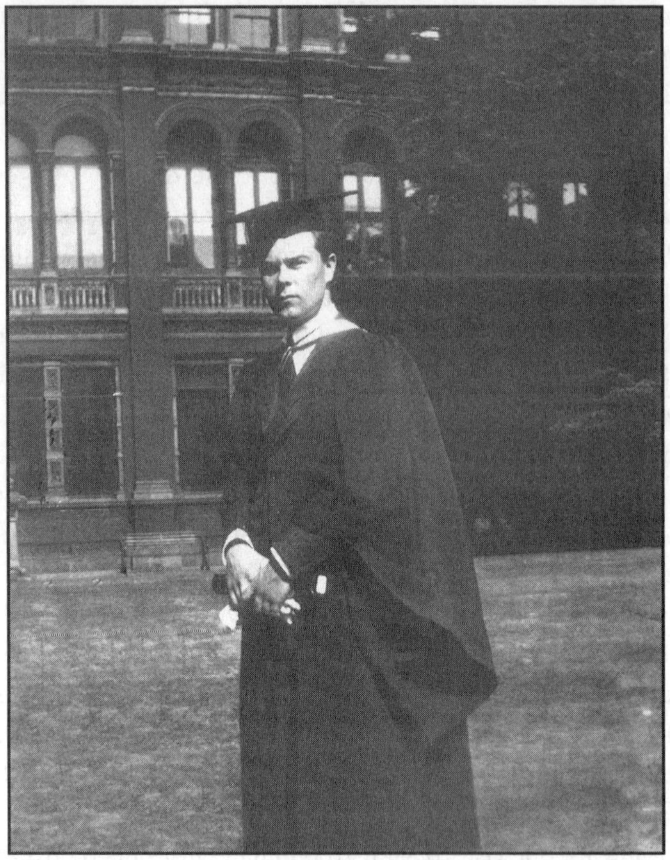

Convocation, a great day, even if it looks grim in this photograph of me

I returned to finish my year in the etching and engraving school at the Royal College.

During Eileen's final year she took a pedagogy course at the Courtauld Institute and Goldsmith's College. The friendship with which our meeting began grew into something more permanent. Eileen had established herself in digs in Redcliffe Road to which I went on Wednesday afternoons, a substitute for Saturday when I did a session of sports supervision like umpiring at cricket matches. On these Redcliffe Road visits I often found a still life set up with instructions to get the painting down by my return. We held our first exhibition in this house.

After the consolidation of our relationship I was invited by her father and housekeeper to a performance of *The Mouse Trap* – I was to be vetted and from then onwards things progressed until I contracted tonsillitis and was put to bed in the guest room. This cemented our relationship and just before war was declared we got married, as did Eileen's father and Bee, the housekeeper. We all eased ourselves into two taxi cabs with four gas masks, making for the nearest Registry Office. We retired to 'Glen Gairn', Eileen's home, for a very simple wedding breakfast shared with my mother. Because of mass evacuation from London we were able to rent a flat in Brompton Road, close to the Oratory and almost opposite

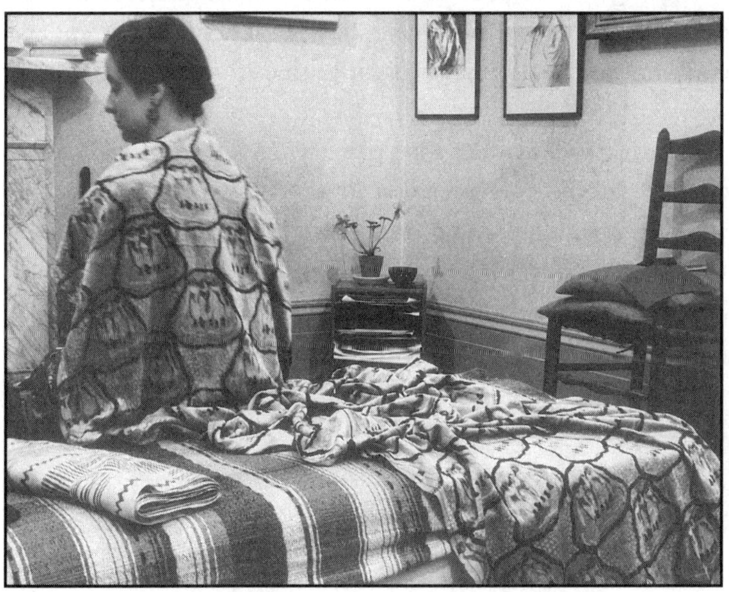

Eileen's digs was the venue for our first exhibition

Harrods for two pounds per week. The wedding was the simplest. Eileen had gone up to a Lyon's 'corner house' and purchased a selection of items from a limited number available, to provide us with a wedding breakfast!

The flat below ours was occupied by a much bejewelled, flamboyant clairvoyant. During an air raid as we stood cheek by jowl under the stairs she said to us, 'This house is safe and will not suffer from air raid damage'. I was not convinced and pending my call-up papers decided not to leave Eileen in London. Shortly after moving away from London we learned that the house we had occupied was the only one to be demolished from top to bottom by a direct hit.

It was in that flat we had had our first burglary experience. Eileen's engagement ring, a large Peridot was stolen, never to be replaced.

Food was becoming difficult to buy. The war years were producing serious problems. A MacFisheries shop at the end of the terrace sold cods' heads cheaply. These we found very economic as they supplied us with fish cakes, and the cat with supper.

A rather sad incident took place when our cat, turning lascivious eyes on a pigeon's nest in a plane tree, just under the window, misjudged the distance and fell onto the pavement. In spite of frequent visits to the vet, he eventually died of his injuries. This was our last cat. We have had dogs ever since. They will come into the picture in due time.

IV
THE WAR YEARS

So we moved out of London into one of a row of minute cottages formerly used by hop pickers from London. These 'Shinecroft' cottages were *small*, very small, but they served a purpose as we shall see. Inevitably, my calling-up papers arrived. I was no longer in a reserved occupation but in the British Army. No longer in an ivory tower! So my army career had begun! I was sent down to a transit camp in Exeter in wintry, cold weather and my first job, sitting in the snow, was peeling swedes. At night we had guard duty. I remember standing before a Nissen hut in my new uniform, complete in tin hat and rifle, feeling like a sitting duck for any sniper. Training was no soft option. To watch officer cadets being drilled by a regimental Sergeant Major on the deserted main road was intimidating in the extreme. They were almost out of sight when they got the order 'about turn' which they did like robots.

Basic training at last came to an end and I was drafted to an anti-aircraft unit in Northern Ireland. The Sergeant Major was a vindictive pig. Most of the unit were from a volunteer group he seemed to favour. During a training keep-fit exercise I slipped on the wet grass tearing a piece of bone off my right knee which resulted in me being transported to a military hospital in Belfast for plaster treatment. The irritation on my leg was insufferable. All I could do was to use a wooden ruler to squeeze in between the plaster and my leg to scratch the itching skin. On my return to camp, this delightful character of a Sergeant Major wanted to put me on a charge for malingering. I think he was peeved because Eileen had accommodation in the same cottage as his wife. I was beginning to learn something about people. Looking back on that first posting introduced me to a very mediocre group of men and I was pleased to pass on.

Having a commission in mind I made the appropriate application and was interviewed by the Brigadier who offered me a place in the unit being trained for the infantry and motor transport. This offer I turned down and returned to camp. Shortly after this event I had a pleasant, well, not quite pleasant, invite to an Officer Cadet Training Unit (OCTU) in Kinross. This was an experience! The barracks had been established for the training of a guards' unit for the first world war. It began to rain on my arrival and thereafter it just rained and rained. The duck boarding between the huts were floating but we were expected to go on parade in shining boots just the same. Each unit was furnished with a coke stove on a concrete base. The stove had to be polished, the base blankowed, so the stove was never used. I saw no evidence of fuel anyway!

Then came a technical test – we had to make a drawing of the mechanism of a machine gun. This was just up my street and I enjoyed the exercise, particularly as it led to another posting in the south. The OTCU training suddenly came to an end and I was sent to the School of Military Engineering in Sharrow, Yorkshire. This was a splendid decision on the part of the Officer-in-Charge in Kinross as it put me into a small class with highly qualified instructors, totally concerned with architecture and sanitation. I settled down very happily with much to learn and I started a notebook of carefully drawn sanitary fittings which I saved, brought home, and had until joining the staff of Chislehurst and Sidcup Technical School for Girls. I lent it to one of the seniors, Una Collins, and never had it returned. The billet in Sharrow was a very well built country house, the marble staircase and other features suggested the late nineteenth century as being the building date. Here I had a narrow escape.

The house had quite a long gravel drive, sloping up from the road. I borrowed a bicycle with the intention of going into Ripon. So I set off down the drive, gathering speed I attempted to use the brakes, especially as I saw the main road getting nearer and nearer. But there were *no* brakes and in a matter of seconds I shot across the road, hit the hedge, and as if I had been propelled from a catapult, went over the hedge, landing in a shattered heap in the field. I was too dazed to remember how I clambered over the hedge, and wheeled the bicycle back to barracks. I did not get to Ripon!

Shortly after this escapade we all moved into the main buildings in the city, consisting of a complex collection of wooden bungalows. I shared an office with two other draughtsmen and we got on well. I played chess with one of the two. We used to walk into the city (into a Navy Army Air Force Institute (NAAFI) I suppose it was), but we found all we needed – a quiet corner, a little refreshment and time. I often lost at chess – there were times when a game went on for several evenings, but we found them very relaxing.

It was in the two and a half years spent at the School of Military Engineering (SME) that I produced a number of

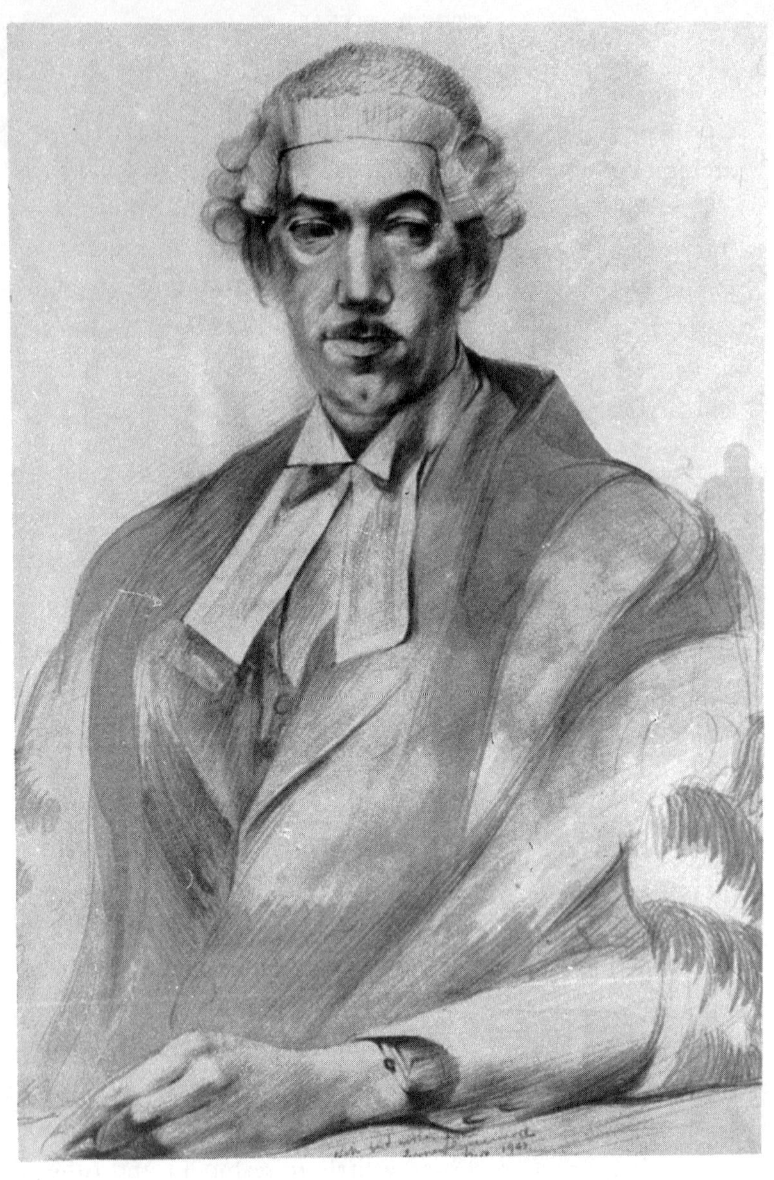

The Town Clerk, Ripon, Yorkshire

Pencil & Wash. 1941. Private Collection.

portraits including one of the Officer-in-Charge of the school. I thought it was a passable drawing and a good portrait for which he did not even thank me, rank dictated behaviour in every way.

It was in this office that I made the large group of portraits, six foot by four foot, in pencil and wash, now in the Stocks Gallery in Suffolk. It was taken with three other works on sale or return. A few other portraits, 'The Town Clerk' – Ripon and several more – in the photographic album record these years.

The time I served in the SME was in the main pleasant. The small city of Ripon was delightful; the cathedral particularly interesting because of the strange plan which shows a faulty alignment between nave and choir. In the square and almost opposite the precincts, was an antique shop owned by an elderly lady who showed charming old-world courtesy. It was in her shop I bought our dining table and a chest to commemorate the birth of our daughter, Dorelia. When I said I was due to go to France any time she said with every conviction, 'You will come back I'm sure'.

It was in Ripon that a number of exhibitions were held by a number of artists working in the school. It caused quite a sensation because I had exhibited a picture in the pointillist style, featuring a nude female!

The abbeys in Yorkshire were a most moving sight, especially Revieux in a vale, like a gem in a rich setting. The centre of culture and agriculture were the abbeys. In their heyday they must have been just wonderful establishments. It is difficult now to imagine the richness of the life their monks lived and fostered. Inside the building complex the monks worked consistently on many tasks. They formed a small fraction of the community who could read or write. They must

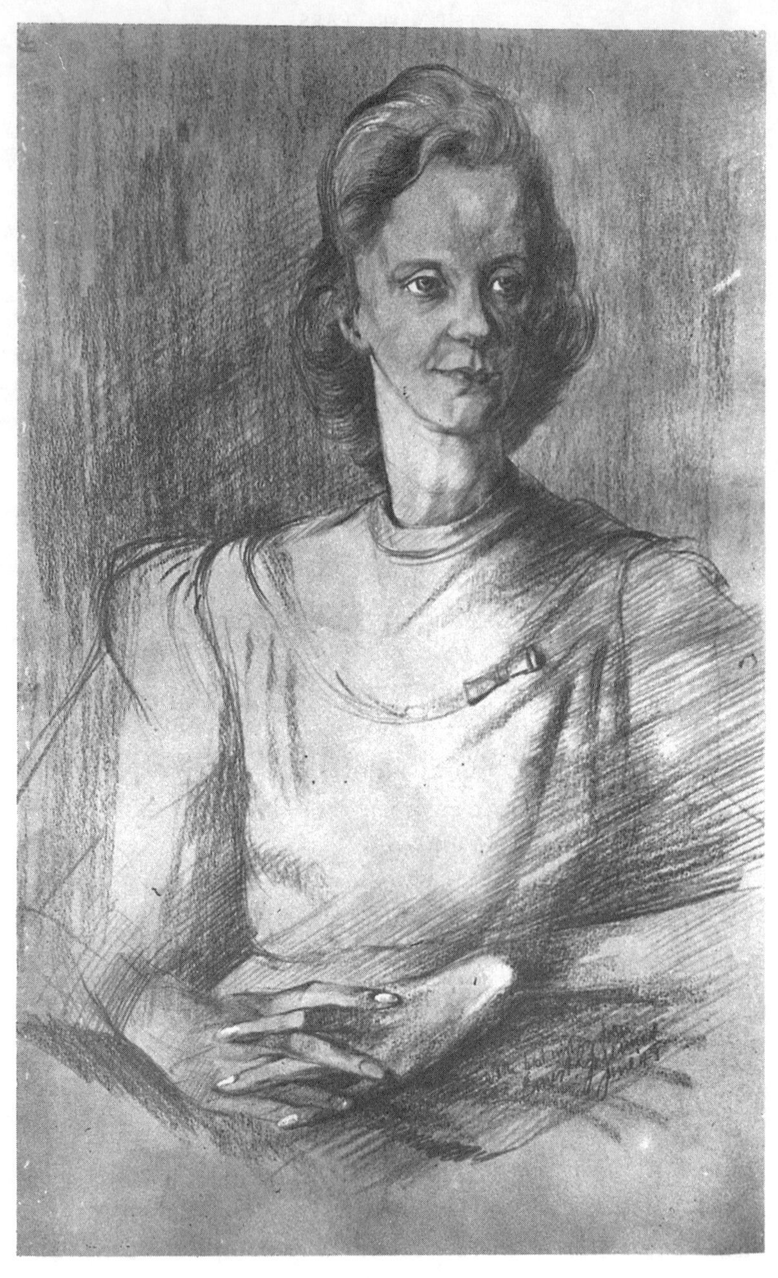

'A Yorkshire Lady'

Pencil & Chalk. 1942. Private Collection.

have drawn up documents relating to wills and inheritance apart from the beautifully written and illustrated Books of Hours. There would have been many travellers on their way north or south, stopping for bed and breakfast and a stable, bringing news of home and foreign parts. The lay brothers would have been busy with large herds of sheep at sheering time, packing up the fleece for transport to cities like Florence, who specialised in dyeing and fine weaving cloth in turn to be exported to the near east. Fountains Abbey is the most complete. The architecture is powerful, confident, rather like Durham, but in its ruined state retaining much of its previous splendour.

My associates were good pals, but never became friends. I did make lasting friends in my next posting which was to 159 Company of Royal Engineers (CRE) in Wilton Park (Ron Marsh and Pat Viner remained correspondents with whom I exchanged visits for many years). I worked in a small office with a mixture of civilian and army personnel. The senior civilian, a man well into his forties, took a fancy to me and invited Eileen and me to lunch at his house to meet his wife and young son. They never seemed to have overcome the shock of being parents, judging by the way they treated the little boy. The phrase so often heard and never to be forgotten was 'eat it all up little man!' None of us had much to do, least of all the Captain in charge of the unit so he asked me to do him two favours. He was a keen fisherman and got me to make an accurate watercolour painting of a trout he had caught in an unspecified river (or bought at MacFisheries). This being done to his entire satisfaction he then introduced me to my second task.

On his retirement, he said it was his intention to live in a semi-bungalow or small house by the sea, and would I design such a type of building for him? Having nothing better to do I set about the job and produced drawings of plan sections as well as elevations and balcony, providing a good view of the sea from his bedroom. Three years in the SME had given me the necessary knowledge. I enjoyed making the designs which he took away without acknowledging the value of my war effort on his behalf! Life in the CRE was very relaxed and in many ways was un-army-like. I had sufficient freedom to live 'out' so I took the opportunity to have Eileen and Dorelia to stay with me. A chance solution for accommodation came when I discovered an old caravan which, judging by the faded text, God is Love, painted on each side, had once been used by an itinerant preacher. This was standing in a meadow that was part of, and not far from, Wilton House. This short-lived sojourn was a very happy time spent in warm, balmy autumn days. The meadow produced an enormous quantity of mushrooms, many of which Eileen picked. She and Dorelia went home when my departure for France became imminent. It was on the back of that caravan that I worked on a watercolour, six foot by four foot, the subject being the resurrection. The good quality army cartridge paper has done well to last so long, but this, now fragile work, nearly seventy years old is rolled up in a yellow Kodak box and lodged at Bonhams. I wonder what its fate will be.

The three of us, Eileen, Dorelia and I, lived in the caravan for some weeks before inviting Bee and Father to visit us. To our surprise they agreed, just for the weekend. This meant giving up the caravan while we slept in a borrowed tent. The weather was fine, we slept very well until the early hours when a snorting and shuffling round the tent woke us up only to find a bullock with its head through the tent flap, with a look of surprise on its face. Gazing at us, it soon wandered off in a slow, dignified manner, leaving us to get up and prepare breakfast for five. Living in the country, in the 'back of beyond' did not suit Bee and Father and they departed, thankfully, back to suburbia. For us it was a short interim, a delightful period before I rejoined the Brigade, under canvas. It was here that the most dramatic event of the war took place. Most of the force was in bed asleep when the sound of distant aircraft got us out to our feet and onto the grass by which time the noise of many planes over head was almost deafening. They seemed numberless with each machine towing a glider. There must have been thousands of soldiers in the air, moving towards a nameless goal. We went back to our beds in silent apprehension. The second event for me was more pleasant; this was a visit to Wilton House. How it came about I have no idea, but I shall never forget walking into Indigo Jones' double cube room and seeing the Van Dyke full length portraits of the Pembrokes built into the panelling. The visual conception of grandeur was paramount. The painter and architect together had produced a unique work of art which needed study to fully appreciate both parts of the whole.

Embarkation for France soon followed. The English Channel was very rough; some of the troops were sick – Ron Marsh in particular so I carried his rifle ashore as well as my own. Our first night in France was dreadful. The region had been subjected to enormous downpours of heavy rain so that the ground under the tents was sodden. We put anything we could muster under the ground sheets, like brown paper bags – just anything to keep the cold and damp at bay. Daylight brought relief. We got into the motor transport with pleasure and headed for the town of Eindhoven. Before moving on to Eindhoven we stopped for a time in the Belgian village of

Lommel. Ron found, in the small bathroom, a broken-down water heater which he, having a hot bath in mind, decided to repair. He spent many days on the job and as soon as the task was completed we all moved on from what had been a very comfortable billet, and Ron had not had his bath! On one of the numerous stops en-route for Eindhoven an ambulance drew up alongside our truck. The driver was Pam Mothersill. Pam was the daughter of Mrs. Mothersill, owner of the tiny Shinecroft cottages and other properties in the village back home. In the nineteenth-century the Shinecroft dwellings were built to house hop pickers from London. As I have previously mentioned, one of these was our first abode before we moved into Bridge Cottage where we lived for twenty five years.

I still have the small sketch book I carried in my backpack, stained with rifle oil, with a sketch of our cook Bloxham, a cockney humorist, sitting in the back of the truck that proceeded our own.

The defeated, retreating German troops left behind them dangerous and spiteful booby traps, and I became a victim of one. It was my turn of duty to remove the still-in-use blackouts. This nineteenth-century house, consisting of several floors, was quite high as were the rooms we occupied. To take down the blackouts I needed a step-ladder, which in due course I found. When almost at the top, the ladder leg broke, throwing me into the room. This was fortunate, for had it been the other leg, or the ladder had been the other way round, I would have gone through the glass window to my death on the pavement below.

Ron shared with me an enthusiasm for chamber and orchestral music. We were notified of a concert being conducted by Sir John Barbirolli, which we both wanted to hear, but it was in Berlin. For official army duties Ron had a motorbike. We could go on this if I rode on the pillion. This suggestion was carried off so we went. Ron was a very skilful driver coping with all the shell-made pot holes as I held on for grim death. We would have enjoyed the performance had it not been for a member of the audience wishing to let everyone know that he was familiar with the work by humming it through. We arrived back in camp safely, but in the morning, some subaltern put me on a charge for being absent without leave, so at midday, standing to attention in front of the commanding officer's desk I explained the reason for my absence. He was a good sort, asked me if I enjoyed the programme but finished with a warning not to overdo the practice – so a smart salute, three steps to the rear and the offence forgotten!

Many years later when Ron married, Eileen and I were invited to the wedding breakfast, made memorable by the abundance of boiled potatoes! Ron and Ruby moved into a bungalow in Romford where they spent their whole lives in what was, I imagine, a very closed rural community. They were strict non-conformists and found periods of meditation an important part of their domestic and social life. Although they both came to my last exhibition, I am not sure that they really approved of my paintings, especially where the human figure was concerned. Ron played the violin but could not broaden his thinking to grasp the fundamental principles underlying all the arts, particularly the visual ones. Ron died in his sleep in 2004. The shock for Ruby must have been very severe. They both enjoyed a very uneventful, unadventurous, quiet life in which his sense of humour played an important part.

My posting remained, for the time being, with 159 CRE Eindhoven, was where I made friends with John Eden. John was a little man with a ruddy complex. Like many very short people (Ron Dalzell), his personality tended to be overconfident, self-important and, competent in some things, he asserted himself and made a very good position of authority with British Tobacco. After the war we met by chance in Southern France. John and Dorelia got on well and we formed a jolly party, spending some future holidays together. His wife, Polly, a qualified nurse, wanted children. John did not, which clearly revealed the selfish side of his nature. He was self-centred in many ways. In our wanderings in France, we often found texts, inscriptions, monuments and memorials, fascinating in the use of language and how it differed from one region to another.

On one memorial we found the word 'sanglier' (wild boar) used frequently. We had quite recently seen a hotel sign featuring a unicorn. In a sudden spasm of inspired creativity John put the two words together making the word 'sanglicorn'. We rather took to the word and put its use to the vote: should we be the founder members of the Society of Sanglicorns? It was a unanimous 'for'. So although the membership never rose above five, we signed ourselves the Society of Sanglicorns. Polly invented the phrase 'Sanglicorns of the world unite' which she enjoyed using in spite of a nil response. It was on one of these holidays that Eileen became 'Meem'. I know of no explanation for this although I suspect it came from John indirectly. Since then, several attempts have been made to rationalise the name without success. Nevertheless, Eileen has been Meem ever since and it is the only name by which she is known by the grandchildren and great grandchildren. Sadly, John has left us, leaving Polly in a nursing home, but in her last note to us she signed the card, 'A Sanglicorn'. So the fun has gone on for thirty years or more. John even clipped a short length of hedge into the shape of a boar to perpetuate the humour he shared with his friends!

I think we must have made two trips to Holland shortly after my return home from Berlin. The first time was a booking made by Thomas Cook for two inexperienced travellers. We were the two! Cooks booked us into the Amstel, the most expensive hotel in Amsterdam. The menus were far beyond what we had money for so we ate at a nearby establishment for all and sundry rather like a Dutch McDonalds.

But the National Art Museum had *such* treasures to satisfy every aesthetic need. I remember standing in front of 'The Night Watch' unable to formulate any adequate form of expression to summarise my appreciation of such a unique painting. It stands alone (like Shakespeare's work) and throws into stark reality the inane, the course and inept submissions for the Turner Prize which have received so much official recognition at the Tate.

It was probably through music that I met the Brederoders. He was first violin in the orchestra. She had a fine voice and sang. The mother and daughter both survive in the photograph album of my drawings and paintings. They were very hospitable. I had many enjoyable evenings when he played the violin while his wife and daughter posed for me. Major Brederoder paid a visit to Bridge Cottage with his sergeant batman. I was struck in the great distance he kept from his companion who was so inferior in rank. This visit concluded our relationship and they gradually faded out of our picture as these passing friendships often do.

The war was over. Clearing up the mess had begun. Troops were soon to be demobbed and the army had begun to prepare for this through the Army Education Corps to which I was attached and sent to Berlin. Our billet was a large nineteenth-century house, one of relatively few to have escaped from bomb damage in Schallotenburg. I was sent to join a small group, nearly half of them being commissioned officers, Major Andrew Firth being the senior, but we formed one friendly society. Andrew and I made a lasting friendship. He taught me to drive in the hazardous conditions presented by the bombed and tram-lined streets. Andrew was a solicitor in Otley and paid several visits to Bridge Cottage when sitting his final exams for the Law Society in London. We enjoyed a number of visits to Chevin Close, Birdcage Walk. Andrew was shortly to become an industrial judge in Leeds; a position of which he was well suited. Andrew and his wife Nora remained firm friends until Andrew's death in 2002 when we learned from Simon, their son that Nora's mind memory was failing – a sad end to a long friendship.

Our work in Berlin introduced us all, by vivid photographic means, to the horrors of the persecution of the Jews. The barbarism, the medieval terror inflicted upon these thousands was unbelievable. I was compelled to do something and painted my second 'Resurrection', a panel five foot by two foot three inches, painted in gouache and incorporated a figure from one of the photographs. The work is now in the Ben Uri Gallery, London, with two paintings of Berlin ruins. Quite a collection of my drawings made at that time are now in the John Stocks Gallery in Bungay, Suffolk. Our short stay in Berlin was made very comfortable by the presence of the original occupants of the house, Herr and Frau Bork. They were a delightful old pair. She was a magnificent cook and made a splendid job in the use of the army rations. I often wondered what they thought of having to cook for British soldiers who I think and hope were courteous in such changed circumstances for them.

At last, demobilisation papers came and we could look forward to going home for good. This last journey was not very luxurious. All the windows had been blown out during one of Berlin's many air raids. As far as I can now recall, the return home was made in an uncanny silence as we all wondered what the future would be for us as we thought of home, our wives and children for whom the souvenirs and gifts had been collected now in our kit bags on the luggage racks. I had bought from an antique dealer somewhere in Holland (the Hague, I think), a large ceramic bowl which I thought was Chinese. On reaching home I had it dated and authenticated by a keeper in the Department of Eastern Ceramics as a genuine example of sixteenth-century Swottoware. However, the decoration showed quite clearly that it had been cleaned too often with fine sand. Nevertheless, it is a treasure to have and to use as a fruit bowl at home.

The war was over, I was back in Otford, but the army experiences had made a different man of me. I had learned a great deal about humanity which I could well have done without. Army and domestic life are poles apart, about the latter I had a little time in Brompton Road or Shinecroft to gather the necessary requirements for dealing with the changing world that was developing around me now. It was probably on the disagreeable last journey back to the embarkation port on the way home that I knew the 'ivory tower' had never received so many direct hits as it did during the war so that the whole edifice had disintegrated. A new and more permanent structure for the future had to be built. Eileen had signed a contract with Eyre & Spottiswood to write two books for the 'technical section'. It was interesting for Eileen to write and for me to illustrate, making an important beginning to the new life ahead.

One of my official visits when working for the LCC was to a secondary girls' school where I was introduced to the headmistress, a Miss Viner, who, it later turned out, was a relative of my friend Pat from the CRE at Wilton Park. Pat was an undemonstrative man I got to know slowly, not much before he was demobilised for medical reasons. He returned to his father's farm which was in need of a young man to inject energy to the business; Pat did this in full measure. Our first visit there took place when taking a holiday in Berkshire, as it was then. Pat recommended a hotel, The Rose Revived at Bablockhithe. My remaining memory is of a small bedroom window with a fluttering chintz curtain of pale pink roses. Our short stay there was very pleasant. The next morning we drove to Littleworth to see Pat, his wife, Peggy, and of course the farm. This was a delightful experience. Pat and Peggy were perfect host and hostess, assisted by the grey parrot, Joey, who lived into old age to delight the family. Peggy told us of the parrot's power to imitate the human voice when one of the children had whooping cough – if Peggy was in the garden coping with the hens the parrot would start coughing to alert her.

Their day began very early to do the milking in readiness for the Milk Delivery Marketing Board collection. During our visit Pat was gathering straw following the grain harvest. I went into the field to help load the transport with bales but I soon found how fit you had to be to keep this up all day. Pat was an expert and did the work with minimum effort.

Our stay was delightful, with many new things to remember, such as our dinner of roast goose (a dish I had for the first and last time), as was Pat's happy optimism. Pat was a good correspondent but infrequent. The farm took up all his time with little to spare. I have kept some of his letters which reflect his poetic appreciation of the countryside. Like Richard Jeffries he could record an incident and imbue it with colour and reality. For example, Pat was cleaning a ditch one day and standing on the bottom he paused to watch some field mice cavorting on the bank which was a delight for him to remember and pass on to me. He is also an excellent craftsman and for a number of years made us a Christmas gift out of wood which he used with considerable knowledge. Our candle holder and box are two prized possessions of his expertise.

But after many happy years together Peggy fell ill with a disease which left her paralysed; a dreadful thing, especially when Peggy had been such an energetic woman. Pat was a devoted and patient male nurse. Peggy's place has been partially filled by the love of his daughter Jill gives by visiting Pat twice a day, setting a wonderful example to others.

V
VOTTY BACH

THE WAR YEARS FALL INTO TWO PARTS as many of the important events took place during my period of leave. It was because of Edgar's marriage to Susan that we were introduced to a village called Cyffylliog in Denbyshire, North Wales, and were told of a vacant cottage to let on the mountain side. At the time we were considering indulging in a telephone for two and six per week which was the amount Willy Jones was asking for rent. So which shall we have, phone or cottage? We chose the cottage. On hearing of our venture, relatives and friends supplied us with all sorts of essentials, but not the beds. We slept warm and snug on our straw palliasse.

Water came from a spring on the hillside. It was probably the purest water we have ever drunk. We learned to use the brick cloam oven for baking which was attached to the end wall of the cottage. Hanging over the kitchen range was a cauldron. Our 4-10 shotgun supplied us with protein – there were many rabbits that never failed to enrich our delicious stews produced by such simple means. A barn was built up against the end wall of the cottage which made a good studio

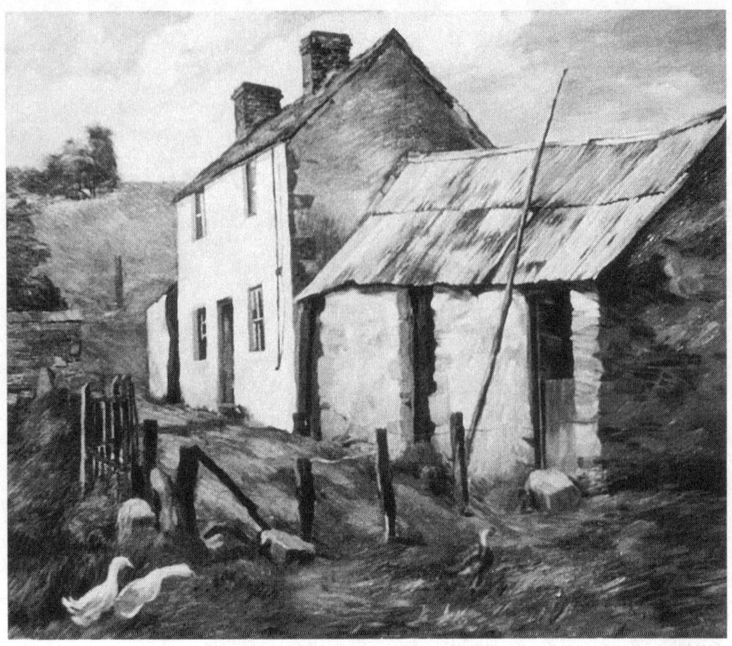

Votty Bach – now a heap of stones

and workshop. Here Eileen carved a torso in oak, a version of which was eventually exhibited in the Kensington Art Gallery. But, because she found a death watch beetle in the first carving she destroyed that work, which after so much chiselling and labour did not please me. We have been over hasty: both of us destroyed work which in hindsight we should have saved. I'm thinking now of the novel *The Strange Emerging* which Eileen started to write. She completed a number of chapters on a small typewriter brought for the purpose. In fact, a lot of writing was done before she thought it should be read by someone qualified to provide a good assessment. She asked Lucy Beech, Adrian's mother, who was so derogatory – she was critical in the extreme. So Eileen gave up, it all went into the dustbin. I was not too pleased with this either!

Votty Bach gave us great pleasure for some years during our relatively short tenancy. One memorable winter was spent over the Christmas period. On waking up one morning after a chilly night and looking through our little bedroom window we found that the world had turned white under a thick fall of snow, and there, at the bottom of the field, was a fox. We watched him with great interest until he finally disappeared into the wood.

The cottage upstairs consisted of two bedrooms, one on each side of a central staircase. We used the left-hand room, which had no door and was open to the landing. Downstairs, there were also two rooms; the larger one on the left contained the kitchen range. Off the kitchen was a store with a stone bench and shelving. From the rafters were large hooks, no doubt for game and meats. This store had a surprising low temperature which we found useful for our perishable food-stuffs. In the winter the kitchen was the only area which kept warm from the range. This amenity needed fuel. The only coal merchant was in Ruthin, to whom we had to go for a necessary supply. During the negotiations with the merchant we noticed a Welsh dresser standing at the back of the shop covered with the dust and dirt of years. We asked about it. Yes, it was for sale, we could have it for ten pounds and he would deliver it with the coal! It duly arrived in two parts, unprotected from the coal and rough mountain ride which it certainly had. The dresser was placed against the only wall large enough to take it as we inspected our purchase. It must have been in that shop for years. The timber was as dry as dust – something had to be done. So, I mixed two thirds of linseed oil with one of pure turpentine and began painting the back. The very wide boards of oak soaked up the liquid like blotting paper. After several coats we began to see some life returning to our dresser. This treatment was followed by Cuprinol, applied particularly to the bottom of the soft wood drawers, although there was no sign of woodworm at all. The result was truly remarkable as its present condition shows. We have since found ourselves in possession of a beautiful and valuable piece of antique furniture which has graced the sitting rooms of all our places of residence. It is one of the treasures we saved from the sale of so many.

Eileen never considered herself a knitter but in a burst of uncharacteristic enthusiasm she knitted herself a jumper. For some unknown reason one of our journeys north left us penniless in Denby. We had the bright idea of going to the police station to see if they would lend us a small amount of money to enable us to buy some lunch. After some questioning and side looks at one another on the reception desk they agreed to lend us two and six. We received this gratefully and in due course returned it with a small donation to a Police Benevolent Fund. This marked the longest walk we have ever made, from Denby to Ruthin. This was quite a walk, nearly too much for our feet, but more than enough for Eileen's jumper. She was carrying on her back a small backpack but the perspiration trapped in the wool of the knitted garment caused it to shrink. On arriving at Votty Bach it had to be peeled off like felt and was never worn again.

It wasn't long before we discovered that the Milk Marketing Board collected the early morning milking from a gate leading into our field. An early visit to the churns with a jug gave us the creamiest addition to our breakfast cereal. Had Willy Jones known he would have charged us for it! One of the most potent examples of the wasteful attitude of this man was revealed when he lent us the pony, Floss, and a beautiful trap – a perfect museum piece. Floss, grazing contentedly, had no wish to work by taking us to the village shopping. She was difficult to persuade even with the help of a bucket of nuts, but we managed. The following was in the spring. We found another trip to the village necessary and therefore needed similar transport. Catching Floss was even more tricky, but when we went for the trap, we had a shock. It was ruined as it must have been used for taking milk churns to the MMB collecting place. The upholstery was torn to shreds, the body work, likewise the former bright paintwork, was faded and chipped. The harness for Floss was in a similar condition, tied up with string, everything showing a complete indication of neglect. In this ill-treated equipage we somehow made our journey to the village and back as it happened, for the last time. The feckless and mean attitude was shown most clearly when one evening we called only to find the farmer's poor, thin wife, Harriot, darning socks by the light of one candle, with the rest of the kitchen lost in gloom. We heard later on that Harriot had died.

At the bottom of our field in a wood clearance we found a waterfall of about nine or ten feet high. The water fell into a small basin before running away down hill. We thought this would provide us with a shower. Putting on warm clothing over our swim gear off we trundled for a refreshing shower. We were two young people in their late twenties prepared almost for anything, but this spring water beat us. The water was freezing, after a minute or two, or less, we put our warm clothing on to combat our shivering. We were goose-pimpled all over and enjoyed the walk up hill to Votty Bach with enthusiasm and relief as our circulation returned. In the first chapter I made a reference to walking! If you didn't walk you stayed where you were . . . Eileen and I were good walkers.

One of my army leaves was spent at Votty Bach. Travelling

by train to Ruthin, stopping at Crewe, I had travelled a long way from Germany and was tired. I took off my army boots and fell asleep. Eileen told me I woke up suddenly on reaching Crewe, where we changed trains, and got out of our carriage in haste, carrying my boots. The walk from Ruthin to Votty Bach was a long one. We had our pet cat with us who walked some distance, but gave up after a mile or two, so I picked him up, made him as comfortable as possible with his head out of the half closed haversack and so he travelled, happily enough, to Votty Bach.

Our nearest neighbour was a farmer working a smaller farm than Willy Jones. We always received a warm welcome when calling. We had a whim that a duck or two up at Votty Bach would be an extra interest for us, so our friend at 'Hindre' lent us a pair. To keep these birds happy we sunk a galvanised bath into the ground just far enough to form a mini pond which they very much appreciated by our temporary lodgers, who looked a most amusing sight when they took it in turns to have a swim. These pastoral weeks we had each year were terminated by an unfortunate incident. We quite forgot to send Willy Jones the rent for the period when it was due. This resulted in a vituperative letter from Willy accusing us of refusing to pay what was due to him. We both had a feeling he did not care for the English, which in one sense was confirmed when we retuned to pack our few belongings. We found a dead sheep in our spring water and an uninhabitable cottage. Jones had allowed the sheep in; the place looked derelict and soon to revert to a pile of stones. We were both saddened at the sight for we had spent so many happy days in that cottage.

Bridge Cottage – Coopers' paintings

On my return home from Berlin I had a most delightful surprise. When I was a teenager, my two brothers and I enjoyed cycling, sometimes with friends but usually just the three of us. One of these excursions took us through the Darenth valley (made famous by Samuel Palmer) which, at that time, had a number of unspoilt villages. The inhabitants work was still concerned with the land, and not a distant office! All these villages had much smaller populations and the last of these was Otford, a few miles from Sevenoaks. On this particular day out we went through Otford, stopping on the bridge to admire the view. It was *so* English: the Oast House, the large eighteenth-century red-brick house, the clear unpolluted river teeming with wildlife which was enchanting. But what caught my attention was the seventeenth-century house with its garden running down to the river. I remember so well the front door being open and painted green. Inside was a small cabinet in an equally small porch. I kept looking at the scene in front of me, at a picture of English village life which has now become a commonplace subject for photographers both professional and amateur. But for me in the 1930s, it looked just wonderful, and I said to myself, I would love to live in that house.

During my enforced absence in Germany Eileen heard that Bridge Cottage, or rather half the house facing the river, was to let. We were then in the Shinecroft property owned by Mrs. Mothersill, who also owned Bridge Cottage. Eileen negotiated with Mrs. Mothersill's agent, who asked a number of impertinent questions regarding our ability to pay the rent. He was a tall thin man who used to cycle through the village closely resembling Dickens' Scrooge. Eileen was convincing enough and moved our few belongings into Bridge Cottage – the very house I had seen and coveted all those years. From then on it was to be our home for twenty-five years. This was the 'great surprise' and our delight for many years to come. So the time had come for me to contact the antique shop in Ripon to tell the delightful, old lady, that her predictions had come true and I was well and at home. I was therefore ready to receive my dining table and chest. They came in perfect condition to serve our needs for many years, in fact up to the time we left for Brushings Farm House.

I never returned to the grammar school. I was invited to join the staff of a newly established Technical High School for Girls. Eileen had already been invited to start a craft department so when I joined Eileen and I worked in tandem, but not for the last time. My five years teaching in the school were very satisfactory. I was the only man on the staff and was treated most courteously by the others and those I taught. These years were memorable for two other reasons. There were on the staff a number of specialists – a musician, a speech and drama expert, a dress-making department, art and craft.

An afternoon was devoted each week to a work which entailed all five disciplines. The Christian festivals of Christmas and Easter became focal points around which ideas gathered and formed the basis of the first and subsequent productions. These dramatic performances reached a high standard, not only because of the quality of the instruction, but also by reason of the serious and sincere attitude of the performers. They were young and believed in the parts they were playing. Having worked as an assistant for Alan Sorrel at the Royal College, I tended to work on a large scale and I hoped to have the chance of completing a scheme as Alan had done, sometime in the future. I therefore looked on the

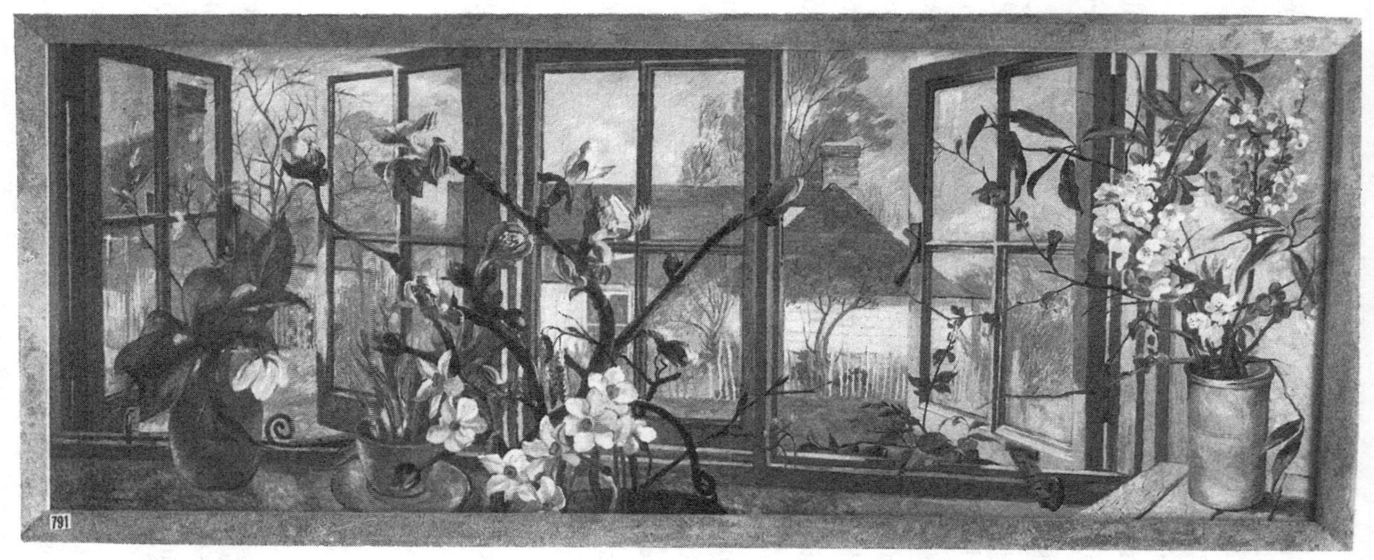

'Easter Morning'

Oil on canvas. 1948. Private Collection.

prospect of decorating the small room at 'Coopers' with great pleasure. The idea was supported by the headmistress and I began designing and painting in 1946.

The room was very light, almost luminous from the high windows and white walls which were panelled in pine about five foot above the dado. These surfaces were just perfect for painting on when using a thin transparent technique. The park was bounded on several sides by old bricked walls and I thought this was a feature which could be used for linking all the panels. There were seventeen panels; two were quite small connecting pieces. I worked systematically for five years. Some of the players posing for me gave a certain authenticity and character to the whole. Many of these portrait studies survived and may be with Russell. I was too optimistic. It is a great mistake to over value your own work or plans for the future because it will only result in disappointment, as they are unlikely to materialise. It was suggested that the Tate Gallery might like to have a set of photographs of this completed scheme to include in their collection of contemporary mural decorations. The letter I have from John Rothenstien, then director, acknowledges the photographs, dated July 11, 1949.

I thought I had produced a complete mural scheme that would be interesting to another generation, but how wrong I was over work I thought was more than meretricious. The paintings were doomed to oblivion.

It was in the 1950s that the Labour government made comprehensive schools compulsory. The technical school was incorporated into a much larger comprehensive for boys and girls and as a consequence, 'Coopers' suffered its first desecration. The charming original interior was destroyed by alterations to accommodate a larger intake. My paintings

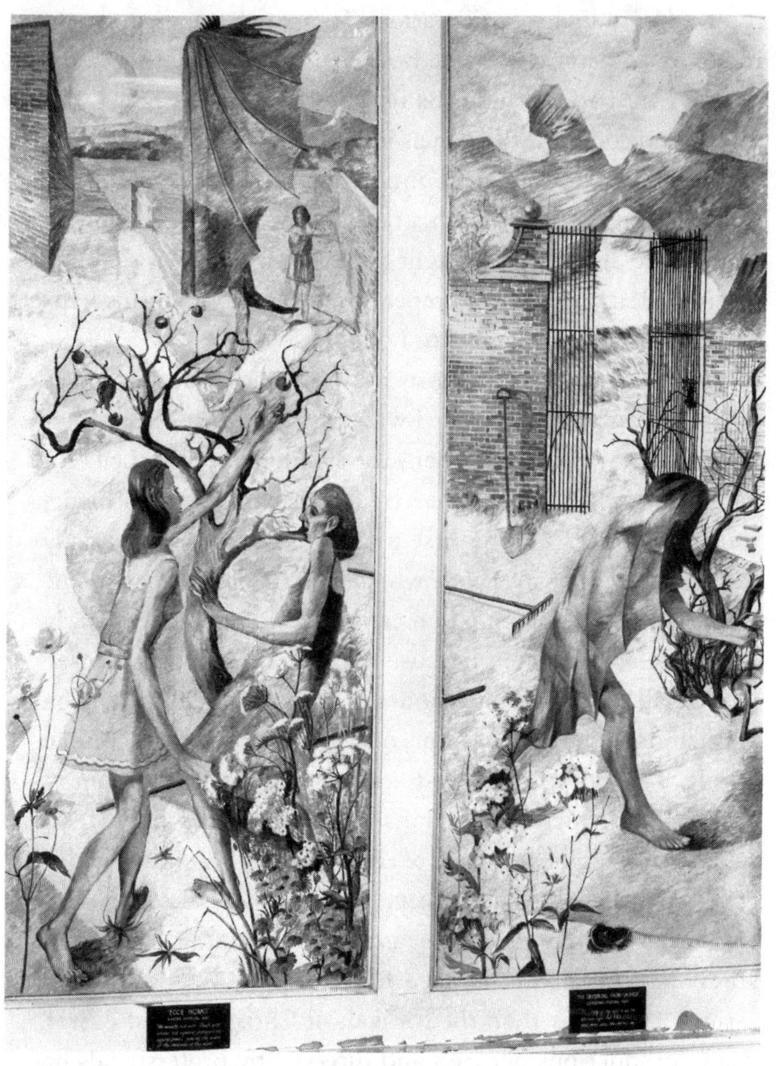

The Chislehurst Murals

A sequence of panels 60' x 8' in a Georgian mansion.
Oil on white painted pinewood. 1950–1955.
Left: 'Adam and Eve'. Right: 'The Expulsion from Eden'.

received very little consideration. The panels were carelessly removed and stacked in the boiler house with coal for company. I heard about these changes by chance and phoned the school and collected the panels in two trips. They were stored at Brushings Farm House until 1973 when they were put into a sale at Sotheby's with a reservation of £600 which was never done. They were bought for £20, of which large sum I received £10. History was repeating itself now! All this happened soon after my move to London.

The paintings were begun in 1946 and completed five years later in 1951, the year I was appointed Inspector of Art Education for, what was then, the London City Council. An agreement was reached whereby my teaching commitments were timetabled for the first four days of the week, Friday being left free for my work which was spent on this scheme and several portraits in oil on canvas. This was a particularly attractive arrangement because the senior school was housed in a small Georgian mansion set in beautiful parkland on Chislehurst Common in Kent, once the home of the Edelman family. The house contained a small pine panelled room of graceful Georgian proportions overlooking the park. This room was ideal for the series of compositions I designed which covered the walls. The subject matter of these decorations was based on an unusual educational programme. The senior students studying music, speech and drama gave two presentations a year based on the festivals of Christmas and Easter. These productions, written and directed by professionals on the staff resulted in original and, in many cases, moving dramas. Cooperation for the decorations from those students involved was most enthusiastic, many of them posed for studies, as in the panel of 'Adam and Eve'. Portrait studies were also made from student and staff, several of which were used in the 'Disputation of the Elders'. A number of these drawing were in the possession of the artist.

For about ten years the room, with its decorations still clean and fresh, remained intact, then came a change. A new education programme necessitated an increase in the size of the mansion and the first floor was gutted which housed the paintings. The administration and their architects, unaware of the unique nature of the paintings, made no attempt to salvage them. All the panels were hacked ruthlessly from the walls, destroying some, splitting others and scratching the surfaces of many.

Information concerning the deplorable treatment and condition in which the work had been left and stored in the boiler house came to me quite by chance. The headmaster, anxious to be relieved of the responsibility, was delighted to have me take them away and stored in my studio until they were sold by Sotheby's in 1979. The agreed reserved price of six hundred pounds was never made and it was with the utmost disappointment that it was subsequently learned that the whole collection of sixteen panels had been sold piecemeal, probably never again to be seen as a complete scheme of decoration in which all the sections had been carefully designed in relation to one another.

The designs were painted direct onto the walls using the oil paint applied thinly like watercolour. The pine wood panels had, for a hundred years or more, been painted white over and over again, producing a high reflective index upon which to work and as a result the paintings looked as clean and fresh as when they were last worked on in 1951 and sold in 1979. As the years passed the paintings were largely forgotten until January 1993. A collector, when visiting Bankside Gallery, noticed that a past President of the Royal Watercolour Society bore the same name as the signature on several of the panels he had collected. This observation resulted in correspondence between myself and the collector; considerable interest was shown in the acquisition and restoration of further sections as soon their location could be discovered and the work acquired. Unfortunately, for reasons totally unknown, the interested collector terminated his contact with me. Since this time one other panel has been located in a North London gallery.

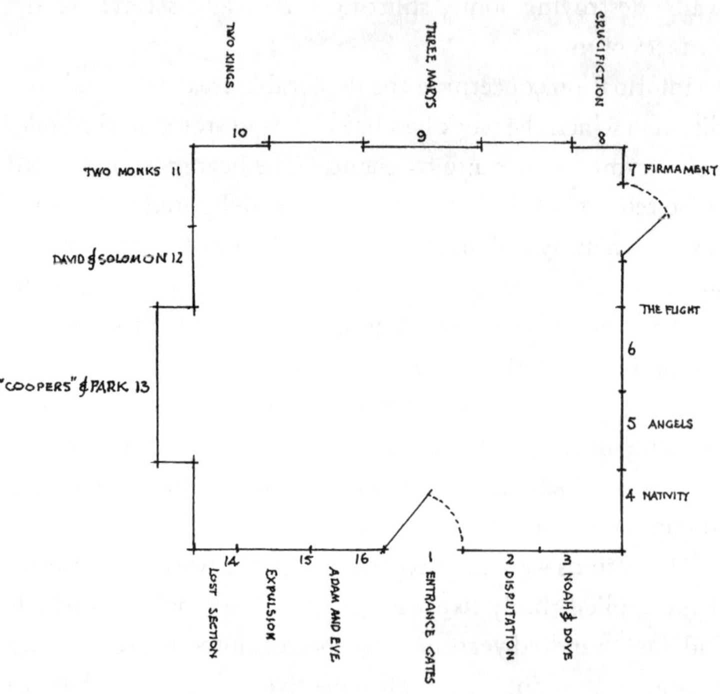

1. On entering the room, above the door, panel one contained a painting of the park gates: across the land, a chapel with two figures leaving the church yard. The linking theme of the park wall begins and ends here.

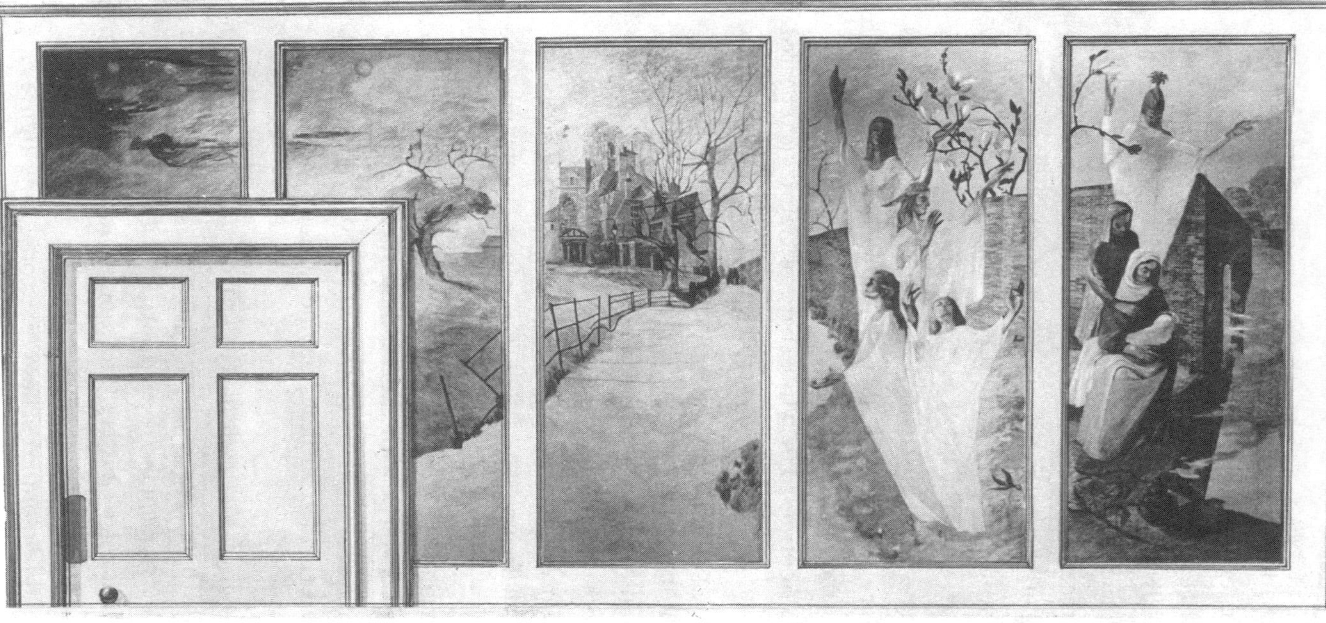

The Chislehurst Murals

Detail of one wall showing panel arrangement. Reproductions of the whole work are held in the archives of the Tate Gallery's 'Collection of English Mural Paintings'.

2. 'The Disputation'. This panel contains a number of portraits of staff and students. Three figures in white silhouetted against the brick walls are here broken into by rafters. Two crouching figures occupy the lower right-hand corner.
3. 'Noah receiving the dove'. The wall continues as a strong vertical on the right of the figure of Noah, repeated in the row of willow trees, reflected in the flood.
4. 'The Nativity'. The flood water ends up against a sharply receding wall against which the figure of Gabriel hovers over Mary, Joseph and child. Their three heads make a foil to the strong white diagonal of Gabriel's robe.
5. 'Angels Adoring'. The white shape of Gabriel is repeated in the four angel's robes counter-changed against the park wall. These figures are portraits of students.
6. 'The Flight'. The park wall continues with the distant figures of Mary and Joseph. This part includes a painting of the now demolished house.
7. 'The Firmament' which suffered badly.
8. 'The Crucifixion'. This small section was closely linked to the 'The Firmament'. Both were probably lost during the demolition.
9. 'The three Marys with the winding sheet'. This was the largest section containing the portraits of three students. The wall theme continues behind a group of rhododendrons.
10. 'Three Kings with a sleeping gardener'. In this painting the wall them is treated with greater variety. In the far distance a horseman is seen approaching the garden.
11. 'Two Monks in a cloister'. One monk standing, one asleep at his desk in the foreground.
12. 'David and Solomon'. These two conversing figures are

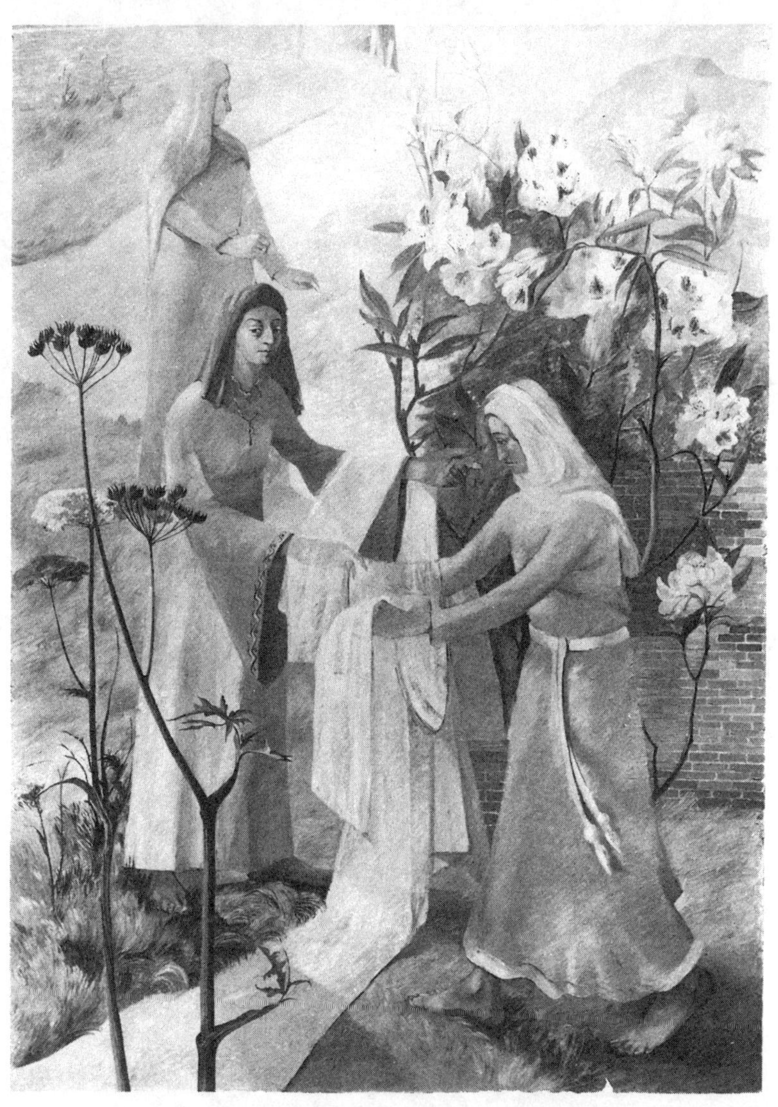

The Chislehurst Murals

Detail of the panel: 'The Three Marys with the Winding Sheet'.

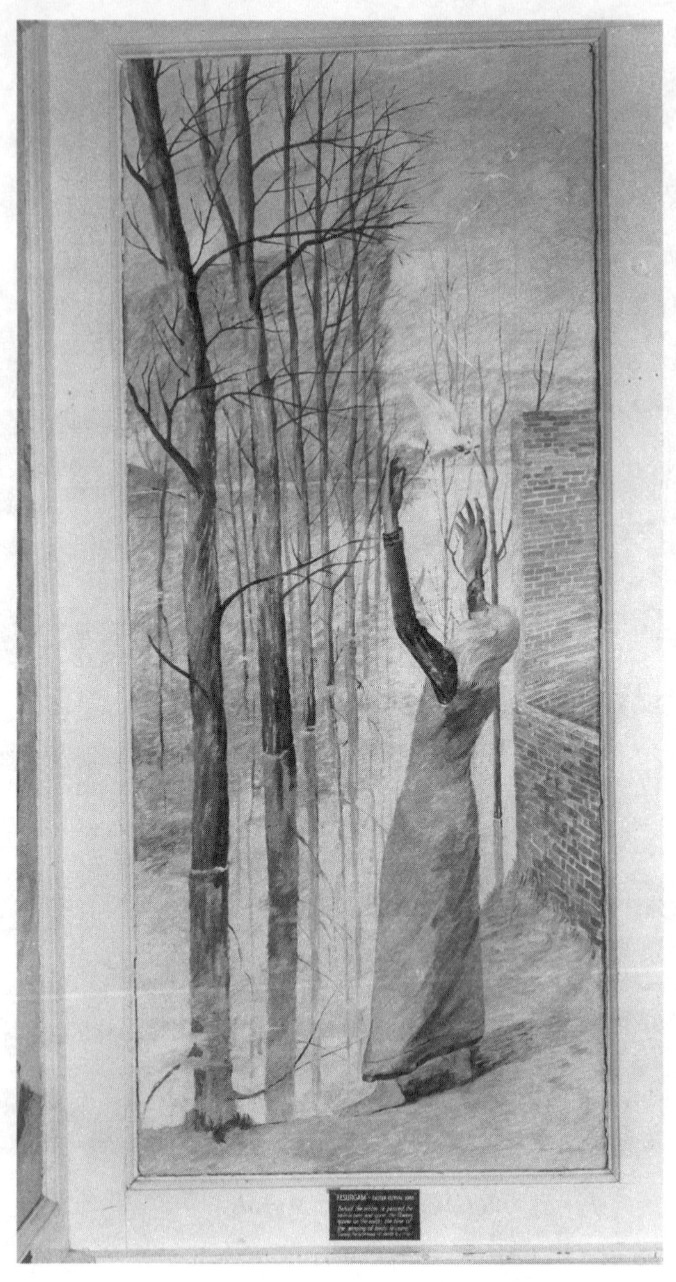

The Chislehurst Murals

Noah and returning dove.

painted with part of the stable block behind which the wall continues.

13. 'Coopers and Park'. This landscape of the house and park covered the space over the fireplace.
14. 'Birds on a fence in a landscape'. This was a linking corner painting now presumably lost. With the exception of this panel I have a complete black and white set of photographs from which any restorations could be made.
15. 'The Expulsion'. The symbolism in this and the preceding panel is more obvious: the spade against the wall, the harsh landscape, the thorn bush, the rake and Adam's garment which is similar to that worn by the spirit of evil in the preceding work.

Is there any possibility that after nearly fifty years, these paintings might again come together and be assembled as a unified scheme in its original form? Unfortunately, although the Tate Gallery has a photographic record of the works, the curator is unlikely to be of assistance in tracing them.

When we first moved into Bridge Cottage the war was still on. Our Morrison shelter covered nearly half of our sitting room but was useful not only for us, but for our red setter who heard the warning sirens before we did. The cottage escaped except for the blast from a bomb that fell some way off. It took tiles from the roof and most of the tiles hung on the façade. Most of the plaster filling between the vertical timbers was shaken and fell in great lumps. Being a timber framed building it seemed as though it shook itself like a dog shaking water off its coat and settled down for another hundred years!

When on leave we often took ourselves off for walks with Dorelia in her pram. On this particular day we were walking through a copse and into a field when we heard the sound of

THE TATE GALLERY, LONDON, S.W.1

VICtoria 6171

11th July, 1949.

Ernest Greenwood, Esq.,
Bridge Cottage,
Otford,
Sevenoaks, Kent.

Dear Sir,

Thank you for the photographs of your recently completed wall paintings at Chislehurst. I should be very pleased to place these on file, although we are not, in fact, taking any active steps to collect photographs of wall paintings.

The rumour which has reached you was based, no doubt, on the fact that we organised, a year or two before the outbreak of war, an exhibition largely photographic, of modern wall paintings carried out in this country. I should have liked to have the opportunity of looking carefully at your photographs, but it is a pleasure which I must, for the present, deny myself, as I am going abroad in a matter of a few hours.

Yours faithfully,

John Rothenstein

Director.

an airplane. It flew very low over our heads and crashed a few yards ahead of us. We were relieved to see a very young pilot jump from the cockpit and run in the direction of the village, leaving his spitfire to be salvaged later.

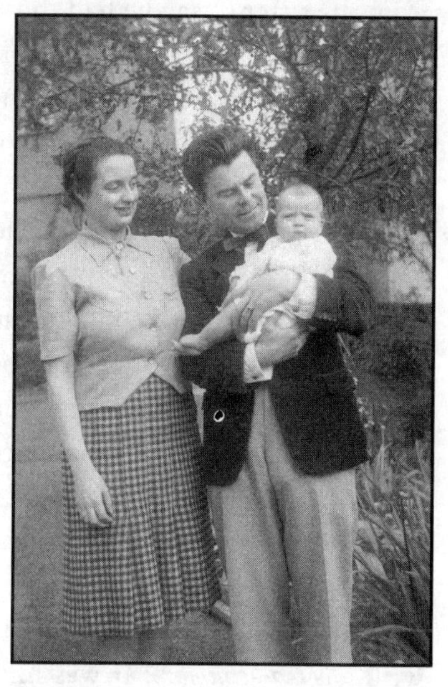

Otford's main and only street still retained a number of shops – a butcher, greengrocery, hardware, baker, chemist (which was opposite the village pond and remnants of a Tudor palace) and, of course a pub. During some alterations to the premises of the Bull pub, three Roundhead pikes were found in good condition, concealed in a cupboard. In a cottage on the main street, which had been neglected for years, was the barber. It was a disreputable, dirty place. Bill Jeffrey did not seem to notice that the cloth he put round your neck was filthy, but he was an innocent character from whom we rented his vacant room as a studio. It served us well. It was in this room I painted the full length 'Portrait of a Dancer', which is now with Bonhams.

Of the several portraits I painted, none ever equalled that of the master of Winchester School, Sevenoaks. The first was painted in a space very close to the boys' lavatory that was not in use as we were working in the summer holiday. The odour was insufferable, but after a sitting or two I completed the job. Shortly after finishing the portrait I had a complaint from the sitter to say he had shown the work to his best friend who said, '. . . it gives the impression that you had a nasty smell under your nose'. But the job did not finish here. I offered to do a second painting if he would come to the studio, which he duly did. He was pleased with the second work, except, I had underdone the colours in, what I suppose was, his school tie! I received the next day an envelope containing his school tie so that I could brighten up the colour! I was concerned with colour-tone harmony.

Following his return home from Rome, Adrian and I maintained a frequent correspondence. He was invited to spend a few days at Bridge Cottage and arrived with a copious amount of art gear. He made a drawing of Dorelia in red chalk – she did not think much of it. Adrian slept in the top bedroom but our loo was down the garden path. He was therefore supplied with a *pot-de-chambre*. It was hilarious to see Adrian tripping along the path with his night contribution held aloft, like a sports trophy, towards the place of disposal. Adrian was not exactly effeminate, but was over precious, which was reflected in the way he responded to some situations or expressed himself in so many ways. During his stay we offered him the studio. It was chilly weather and I suggested he lit a fire. This meant carrying a bucket of coal down the village street, which he did, quite oblivious of the smiles of amusement which followed in his wake.

Adrian lived with Lucy, his mother, all his life, in a small house in Mayford, near Woking. It was grievous to see her senile condition when Adrian called with her at Brushings. Some years afterwards his correspondence began to be ragged and disorganised. He died, sad to say, unfulfilled. Both he and Lucy thought he would be taken up and patronised by someone like Lord Clark, but I could never see this happening. To a large extent, Adrian lived in a world of make believe, of unreality. He lived too much in the past, making his painting eclectic and his drawing unconvincing. He, like many of us, had aspirations, without quite enough ability to realise them. But Adrian was very generous and a good friend to me.

One of the changes we were allowed to make to Bridge Cottage was to move the back door from the sitting room to the kitchen. We could never understand why it had not been done years before we moved in because it made the sitting room warm and cosy and the kitchen more accessible from outside. We also removed the plaster board ceiling and in so doing brought down a shower of straw and dirt. This enabled us to clean and cuprinol the rafters, improving the kitchen appearance.

In the 1940s Otford must have looked the perfect English village. It was certainly advertised as such and stimulated an interest in walks to the area. Trippers from inner suburbia would take the train to Shoreham, walk through the Darenth valley to Otford where they would end up on the gravelled roadway almost in front of our house. Some of the comments we heard, sitting in the garden, were not only original but funny. One of the best was from a cockney who, looking about him said 'I say Bert, I bet the girls in this village wear flannelette drawers', and again, 'Cor, look at that imitation of an old 'ouse'. We had an old quince tree overlooking the river and one said to the other, 'Look at them pears', and in a scornful voice his companion said, 'Thems not pears; thems quinces'. These overheard comments made us feel we were living in a country village while being conscious that Otford, like so many others, had already ceased to be a farming community but had become a dormitory for those working in the towns.

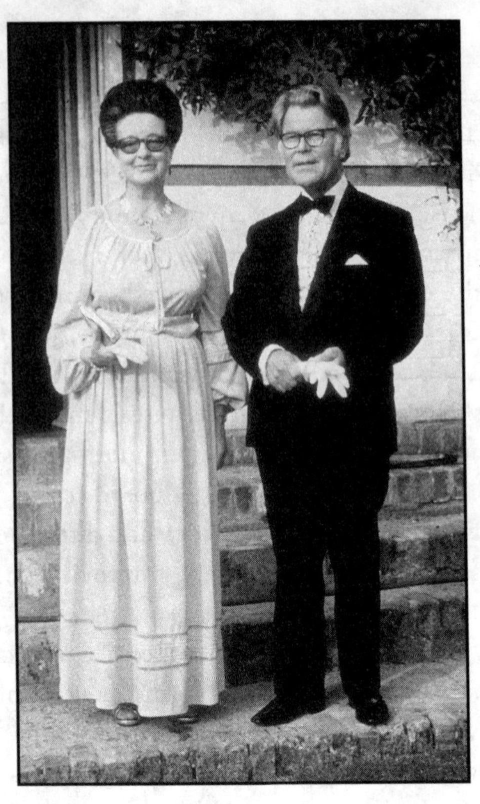

The Lord Chamberlain is commanded by Her Majesty to invite

Mr. and Mrs Ernest Greenwood

to an Afternoon Party in the Garden of Buckingham Palace on Tuesday, the 21st July 1964, from 4 to 6 o'clock p.m.

(Weather Permitting)

Morning Dress or Uniform or Lounge Suit.

One other anecdote that comes to mind took place on a Saturday morning. I was working in our studio. It was a warm day so I had the window over the street open, when I heard the most disturbing racket coming from an infant in a pram. I remember that the wheels were squeaking as an accompaniment to the child's temper. As they passed under the window I heard the infant shouting at the woman pushing the pram, 'You owe me sixpence'. The demands and expectations of the young have increased considerably since then.

Considerable changes took place in our lives during our twenty-five years occupancy of Bridge Cottage. The large manor house was a fine medieval timber framed building with a minstrel gallery at one end. Mr. Rogers lived there with a husband and wife as domestic staff and gardener – the Kilbeys. They had two children, a boy and a girl, who were two playmates for Dorelia when a little girl. Mr. Rogers was interested in cricket and grew willows from which were made cricket bats. This house was almost opposite Bridge Cottage, on the other side of the road, and terminated the old part of Otford.

ꕥ VI ꕥ

WE BOTH MOVE TO LONDON

SHORTLY AFTER COMPLETING the 'Coopers' wall decorations and feeling I needed a change I applied for the post of Inspector of Art Education, South London, then known as the LCC. During my five years of teaching we had won, two years running, the *Daily Mirror* Children's Art Competition. One of the adjudicators was the Chief Art Inspector for the LCC. He paid me a visit, saw the painted room, made no comment and departed. Some weeks elapsed before I was invited to attend an interview during which I was offered the job and remained in the post for fifteen years. These years provided very little satisfaction and there were times when I was sorry I ever took the job. The Art Inspectors and the Inspectorate as a whole were governed entirely by the politicians who were in the process of establishing the comprehensive system in London and throughout the country.

During my visits I saw some of the results of a policy implemented by bigotry and mistaken education theory that all children required the same environment in which to grow. Several small grammar schools with splendid academic records closed and flagship 'Kidbrook' built, but never repeated.

I shared an office with Barclay Russell, Maurice Wheatley and a secretary. My first few weeks were not those I wish to remember. This was the period of 'Child Art' with its vociferous prophet Herbert Read. I was expected to write up a report on the art found in Primary Schools when in the majority of schools, there was none. Eileen helped me fabricate reports after some particularly difficult visits where staff were happy to distribute art materials aimlessly. The children would not get far if the same principle of free expression was applied to other forms of creativity such as music.

Barclay Russell was aloof, very superior, with a long pedigree, but not a colleague one could respect or with whom one could share any problem. He was an eccentric in dress and in the matter of his car. This was in such a state of advanced decrepitude that he was stopped by the police; the result was never divulged. Maurice Wheatley proved to be a shallow character who did nothing to help me into a new job. For a year or two he was all over me, invited me home to meet his second wife, an ex-student of his, asked if I would become his son's godfather, would I help him change his car, and so on. I thought it only decent, on his birthday, to suggest I took him out to lunch. I booked a table at the Shangri La in Brompton Road. At the end of a pleasant meal in lovely surroundings he just said, 'I would rather have gone to a pub!' So . . . he was left to go to a pub. Very gradually it became evident that he was an alcoholic but not so much so as to prevent us inviting him to Dorelia's wedding. He was late. Then I got a call from the Police, 'Did I know a Maurice Wheatley?' So it was left for me to bale him out. Drunk, he had driven his car into a ditch. My expressions of disgust at such behaviour made little impact. He continued to be a slave to whisky until his death.

The most ignoble act of his, however, took place after I had left London and was in Kent. He took time and money motoring down to Brushings to say the Education Officer asked about me and would I apply for the post he was leaving. Now I had grave doubts about this because when I resigned from the London Authority it was apparently customary for the Education Officer, the recently knighted William Horton, to wish the departing officer good luck! I was kept waiting in the office a long time before a call came through, 'Sir William will see you now'. So down I went to his outer office only to be met by a clerk who said, 'Sir William hasn't long you know!' Entering the inner sanctum I was confronted by a smallish man standing by the fireplace. I was not invited to sit. He wanted to know my name. What was my subject? How long had I been with the Authority? So, having worked for him as Education Officer for fifteen years, you can imagine how I felt. It was a complete summary of what I thought and now knew about the GLC. Maurice Wheatley had come down to give me a false message from this man!

This is where I made a big mistake – believing to a certain extent in the message purporting to have come from the Education Officer, I went to the interview. This was my second mistake; but it did reveal Wheatley in his true colours. Instead of keeping his mouth shut which would have been friendly, at the end of an embarrassing situation he asked a very difficult and personal question unnecessarily involving me afterwards, leaving it to someone else to tell me the result.

Following Wheatley's death, Mac (the Inspector of French), Dennis Stephens (who gave me the complete works of John Donne) and I went to the funeral. The parson gave a short, uncomplimentary talk in which he referred to 'this alcoholic'. Mac and I enjoyed a certain rapport: he was to take a second group of teachers of French, ten or twelve, to Strasbourg University and asked if I would join him by taking an equal number of teachers of art, to which I agreed with pleasure. I saw no sense in taking such a group unless they had work to do. I selected a generous supply of art materials and had the lot sent to Strasbourg expecting to find the box containing our supplies waiting for us. Oh no. They were with the customs officer who was suspicious about its contents. Mac and I went time and again with all our precious working session being wasted. By the time the crate arrived, about a quarter of our time had gone. Even so, a very commendable body of work was produced and thinking that the members would be pleased to see the results of their course that had been sanctioned, I told the group we would put the work on show along one of the corridors of County Hall. But no permission was given, they did not want to know. The next year my colleague working north of the river took a group as I had done and he came back with a few photographs including one of Mac holding a glass of red wine! Why did I take such a serious view when so little was required or appreciated?

I left London with a poor opinion of this mammoth political organisation which was, in many ways, a second government who influenced the millions of Londoners. I was conscious of this when summoned to a council meeting (where I was deputising for Wheatley) with education being on the agenda. When a question arose about staffing Kidbrook School I was expected to reply, which I did by saying I had found the right person to appoint. But before I could go on a member shouted, 'You didn't appoint anyone, the Committee did', making me feel small. I had done a lot of work to finalise this. Once or twice a term we had people to interview who were applying for assistance to enable them to pursue a further education course. Our instructions were to recommend any black persons wishing to become doctors, solicitors or teachers, even though many of them spoke very little English. They cannot have been in England all that long!

One of our jobs was to visit the large London Evening Institutes so, rather than motoring home late at night, I joined the Chelsea Arts Club and took bed and breakfast for ten shillings. I only used this convenience once or twice but it was quite an experience taking super at a long table with the President of the RA at the top.

Apart from two large children's art exhibitions during my time with the GLC, I managed to have six or seven one-man exhibitions: Walkers in Bond Street, The Zadler Gallery, Kensington, two in Suffolk, the second of which I must record. Eileen and a colleague from Battersea (I will return to this phase again) worked most professionally, producing the buffet. To this show we invited the Education Officer and a number of senior officers. Without replying to the invitation card the Education Officer (then only Mr!) and his retinue turned up, helped themselves liberally to the buffet, and departed without a word to either of us. You can guess what we thought of such discourtesy. Wheatley bought two pictures for the Circulating Art Scheme. When the clerk came to pay for them he looked up the regulations and found it was illegal for one employee to purchase work from another. So he brought this to the notice of his boss and I was kept waiting many weeks for payment. The clerk got a promotion for his diligence!

One pleasant event occurred in the sixties when I was invited to accept the presidency of the Hesketh Hubbard Art Society. This was a flourishing enthusiastic group of amateurs using the Suffolk Street premises (where I had held two exhibitions) before moving to the Pall Mall Galleries. I resigned on changing my work for the Kent Education Committee. With a sigh of relief I left London for good. The daily two-hour drive was quite a strain especially in the short, dark days. In 1964, when so much snow fell, it was difficult leaving Broad Street as the hamlet was built in a small valley.

On leaving home one morning, when the roads were at their worst, I was negotiating the small hill on the way to Westminster when in a sudden skid into the left hand bank the car turned over. I was able to struggle out and while standing in the lane contemplating the situation who should be coming along but Peter Horton, a neighbour from a nearby smallholding. After exchanging various comments on the situation we decided that to put the car back on four wheels could possibly be helped by the icy road, so we took our places, one in front and one in the rear and gently rocked the car to and fro before making the final heave. It worked, the vehicle dropped onto four wheels, I got in and drove to Westminster, expecting the engine to stall. But no – it took me to London many times before its scheduled servicing took place. This incident confirmed my high opinion of Volvo.

It was a two-hour drive to Westminster (one hour to Peckham and an hour from Peckham to Westminster) which I did, but for a few days by train, for fifteen years. The amount of energy and time wasted and the absence of any satisfaction at the end were making me anxious for a change which came unexpectedly, and was ideal. The year before, in 1964, Eileen was asked by the Education Officer if she would accept the job of founding a College of Education for mature students. Eileen came home expressing grave doubts about her ability to do this, to which I replied, 'If the Education Officer had not been convinced that you could do it he would never have asked you'. After some discussions on the problems inherent in the invitation, Eileen accepted. So she left the inspectorate, leaving a vacant post to be filled. The advertisement was for an Inspector responsible for art only although Eileen had done the work of two: art and domestic subjects. I applied for the post hardly expecting success, as I was over fifty years old, but to my joy and intense relief I was given the job.

Eileen's appointment to Battersea College of Domestic Science

After my departure from 'Coopers' to London Miss Scorrer, the Headmistress, said to Eileen 'he's got promotion, you stay'. She could not have been more wrong. Eileen applied for a lecturer's post at Battersea College of Domestic Science. The interview was very pleasant. Eileen left thinking she would be notified later but a few hundred yards down the street she was hailed by the Vice Principal, Mrs. Mac who asked if she would wait and return to college. On doing so Eileen was promptly offered the vacancy, which lead on to lasting friendships.

The post was only made possible by the 'dyed in the wool' staff surrendering a period or so to art and craft, a move for which they were quite unsympathetic. They saw no reason for the subject anyway, except to be a service to domestic science! So, for Eileen it was an uphill battle but supported strongly by Francis Laidler and Mrs. Mac. So, we found ourselves working in London, Eileen with an interesting job of establishing an art department with strong backing, whilst I was unhappy with the men I worked alongside.

Battersea College extensions took place in what had been a large Edwardian garden. It once had a large brick summer house, but now a ruin. I found it attractive, especially in some lights. I made a drawing which hung about for years – it sold eventually.

Meem did pioneering work in Battersea College of Domestic Science although the staff were opposed to giving the time from their traditional place of prominence in the matter of domestic and hygienic education. What has art got to do with the important subjects we are concerned with, they asked. It was up to Eileen and Miss Laidler to show them and they did! Once ceramic work was underway a kiln was needed. Wheatley had to approve; he paid one of his flying visits and a kiln was delivered. But time ran on and Eileen came to the end of what she could do at Battersea, especially so, as Frances Laidler was near her retirement. Frances retired and with her friend Jane (both were chain-smokers) moved into a small cottage in High Halden. We paid a visit or two and I was pleased to see my portrait of Mrs. Mac over the fireplace.

Thereafter, seeing an advertisement for an inspector of art and domestic subjects Eileen applied; but weeks and weeks went by without any acknowledgement. Eileen said, 'I thought it would be a waste of time'; but I was not so sure. A day or two later Eileen had an invitation to attend an interview to which, of course, she went and was offered the post during a subsequent conversation where it was explained that the long delay had resulted from a member of the committee being abroad. The appointment meant Eileen had to learn to drive. Until then I had done the driving and Meem had been an excellent navigator. So driving lessons were booked and conducted by a most difficult instructor. Nevertheless, Eileen passed the test first time. I think she found the work satisfying but the amount of driving exhausting because Kent's boundary included Bexley, a fair drive from Maidstone.

At this juncture, building extensions were taking place at Springfield. Eileen saw stacks of bricks, seconds for foundations. We were in need of bricks for garden wall construction so a little time spent on chit chat with lots of charm and Eileen's car was coming home daily with a boot full of bricks. It was with these that the wall and arch into the lower lawn area was built.

Alden Miller was the chief inspector, an introspective scholar with a sense of fun, he also wrote verse of which we have a volume. It is very good by the highest standards. He wrote under the name of John Alden but I wonder if anyone will have read anything of his. On one occasion when chatting to Eileen about this and that, holidays were mentioned. She said we were going on a southern France tour to include Couques. He asked what Eileen knew about Couques and she must have enlarged on our interest in Romanesque culture in Europe because this started a friendship which grew into permanence as time went by. Mol, Alden's wife, was very affectionate. She too was an intellectual, a great reader. One year Alden and Mol joined us for a French holiday. They were travelling out by train and we arranged to meet them at the station of Couques which was no mean feat since the line was seldom used judging by all the wild flowers in bloom between the sleepers. They got off the train onto a very little platform and stepped over the rusty lines to greet us. We had a memorable stay in this small village-cum-town famous for its splendid Romanesque portal and treasury. It is a marvel to me that it (the treasury) has survived for so long the depredations of theft and vandalism since the thirteenth century.

I remember the road ran over a lower path leading down to stalls for cows and horses. Leaning over the parapet of the bridge we thought the smell was wonderful. Dorelia referred to it as the country's Christian Dior. It was *very* hot, the steering wheel untouchable if not covered over. One hot evening we were all very thirsty so we found a white wine we all thought was special when chilled. I am afraid we drank several bottles while amusing ourselves by catching the flies which were in plentiful supply from the nearby stalls, and would insist on making the catching of them tantalisingly difficult.

These were the days of our Morris Traveller car. Somewhere we have a photograph of Alden and Dorelia sitting at the open doors of the Morris with their legs hanging over the rear, keeping cool by eating large ice-creams. These exploratory tours in France were just wonderful. They were made before the mad rush of tourism had begun to destroy much of simple, un-commercialised life. Just one example comes to mind. We made two visits to medieval Gordes, one of the few ancient hill towns to survive intact. Our hotel accommodation was of the simplest kind, but the hospitality warm, genuine and generous. I wanted to buy the gate twin towers but events since have shown what a mistake this would have been as the change to Gordes seen on our second visit was painful. A Disney-type train had been installed to take children an easy way to the top of the town. The shops in the market square 'modernised', tarted up twentieth-century vulgarity in advertising and produce-pushing spoke of a new generation who, in my view, were misusing a town which was in their trust for the future. The first sight of Gordes from a distance was breathtaking, perhaps the best view now.

During Meem's time as a member of Kent County Inspectorate she made many good friends, unlike my period in the London Inspectorate when I made none comparatively. Alden and Mol were special in every way, but so were John Haynes (the Education Officer), Harry Broadbent, Bill Petty and others of seniority, of which Meem was one, as time proved. We met socially, organising parties during the winter months which were very enjoyable. They certainly increased Meem's prestige when we were the hosts as this formed one of her many gifts.

Courses for serving teachers were one of the additional responsibilities of the inspectors. The courses were short, from a few days to a week, but were intensive, demanding considerable preparation. Several of these courses, run by Meem, were in Kingsgate in hired premises. Meem being involved with two subjects had, as a consequence, more courses to organise. I remember her starting off for the quite long drive to Kingsgate with the car loaded to the roof with essential gear. This was before Eversley came into being – a large nineteenth century house (once lived in by Charles Kingsley's daughter) that was bought by the Kent County Council and turned into a college for the express purpose of running short courses for serving teachers. The director, an Irishman, was fully engaged supervising the smooth running of a very busy establishment as courses were almost continuous, often extending over four or more days. The catering was good and the service very civilised. You could take a drink from the bar and return to a comfortable lounge before classes were resumed. When the county discontinued this service and the policy of employing inspectors, Eversley was closed. The house was sold and so ended a most valuable support for all the teaching profession. This policy no doubt reduced the cost of education but at the price of doing considerable injury well into the future. The Inspectorate was a highly qualified group of specialists who gave advice and help where needed, especially when student teachers were doing their school practice, or during their first year of full time employment.

This was the time when counties, with government backing needed a university or were persuaded into the need. So the University of Kent was founded and a chancellor was appointed to guide these first years into a vigorous beginning. It was for a number of administrative purposes that Dr. Templeman had to stay in Maidstone for a day or two. Where could he stay? John Haynes, thinking of Brushings Farmhouse, suggested the Greenwoods! So we found ourselves providing hospitality for the new chancellor's wife.

Unknown to Meem her reputation was growing amongst the senior hierarchy and she was seen as the only one suitable to help found Sittingbourne College. Meem came home full of doubts about her ability to do the job. I spent a little while contradicting this notion and so we set about putting a few essentials on paper. So this was just another challenge for Meem! To begin with there was the old Grammar School building, evacuated by the Horticultural College, to be repaired and refurbished, lecturing staff to be appointed, domestic staff, kitchens and grounds men. There was furniture for lecture rooms for staff studies, the Principal's study and administrative rooms to be allocated and equipped, together with a balanced lecture schedule for academic staff. All this and much more before an opening of the college could be fixed. I was the witness and saw from the sidelines most of this accomplished. The college was at last ready to interview potential students and the first enrolled. But there was something missing! I remember some difficulties over chairs. These had been ordered well in advance but nothing came, so a few phone calls were made, but no chairs arrived so more phone calls. I cannot recall who was threatened with what but that night a huge van arrived with chairs which were unloaded and distributed by the staff. These colleges for mature students were established in a number of counties. The purpose was to feed into the profession a number of mature, married people, in most cases with children of their own. As teachers reached retirement and left there were always some mature experienced people to move up into more responsible positions, at this time in the sixties a respected part of the educational system. This was visible in their immaculate dress. No teacher in front of a class would be seen in shirt sleeves rolled up!

From my personal observations I could see what a good thing these colleges were. Sittingbourne College in its ten years of life did a splendid service for Kent Schools. The college had a very large library with a section dealing with children and child education exclusively. The ethos was only made complete by the generous spirit of everyone working towards a common goal.

The college Meem was asked to open had an annexe which only added more work for the Principal. But when the Education Officer asked Meem to open a second one she wisely stuck her heels in. This was expecting too much. There was not the recruitment possible in this area to warrant it. If you want this, she said, it must be by another Principal. The Education Officer capitulated. As you will understand, I had a great admiration for what was achieved. To embellish the college Meem bought from a sculpture student in Hammersmith School of Sculpture, a terracotta seated figure which was considered to be an excellent piece of modelling. The head of the school was a man called Brown, one of Wheatley's way-out, easy appointments. Meem had a little money available and wished to add something comparable so she contacted Brown, reminded him of the previous purchase and arranged a future visit, after suggesting it might be a competitive thing if it was going to entail new work. So the day arrived when we set off for Hammersmith to meet Brown. On arrival there was no reception, no Brown. We were left to find our way to the appropriate studio only to find a number of

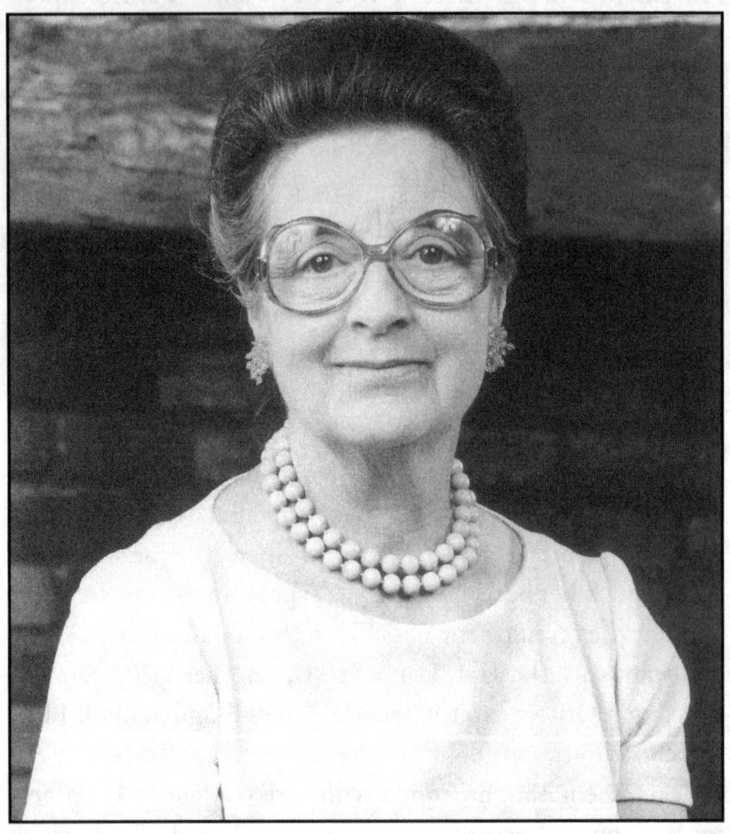

self-satisfied, smug students sitting or standing by their competitive subjects. Most consisted of wire, cardboard, string and paper. They were dull, eclectic objects – there was nothing suitable, as far as we could see. It was the sort of thing they might have done in the back kitchen. We came away having seen no Brown and no secretary. Rather saddened by such appalling behaviour, we heard nothing from Brown. I remember from his few visits to the office his slow, slouching walk with that tired, cold look. Wheatley must have seen this but to install the incumbent saved much trouble! So Meem never bought her second sculpture for her college. What was the fate of the terracotta figure, I wonder?

These colleges were doing an essential work for education. However, according to the then Minister for Education, there were too many colleges specialising in their training and they were no longer necessary. So an edict went forth demanding (with customary political euphemisms) the closure of *all*, not some, but all colleges of education. The libraries, staff – all very qualified specialists – found themselves on the redundant list. The buildings are closed and money has been spent adapting them for other uses. Now the shortage of teachers had become a political issue made manifest by a very short-sighted Minister!

It was perhaps about four years before the closure of the college that I was invited to join the London University Examining teams for the art qualification for teachers in colleges of education. I had a number of colleges, very scattered over a large area of Greater London, as far as Cockfosters. As you would expect, some were better than others! That a few colleges had art students with little talent were left to imagine their work often on a large scale had a real significance. I found the experience of great value as it enabled me to form a balanced view of the relative concepts and principles upon which the Sittingbourne College curricula were based.

So a very wonderful phase in Meem's professional life ended rather sadly, but she quickly turned her attention to another aspect of creativity.

VII
SWAN HELLENIC

OUR EXPERIENCE OF CRUISING began and ended with Swan Hellenic. These adventures had their birth in an old clapped out ship which had lumbered its way round the Mediterranean for too long but carried the most enthusiastic travellers with whom we have ever journeyed. In spite of a complete lack of amenities, for example, all the loos and showers were in one block amid ship, but as far as I can recall there were no complaints. Luxurious travel had not yet removed all adventure from expeditions abroad but this ship *Ankara* was soon replaced by the *Orpheus* – a much more suitable vessel for the task and it was on this ship that we did all our lecturing, with one break with Alden and Molly on the *Meltimi*, a very small vessel in which we could, and did, explore little coves and beaches. It was on an early cruise to Asia Minor at Side that I sat on a slab of masonry to make a drawing. I had not been working long when a shadow fell over the work, looking up I saw Doreen Goodrick watching me. It must have been shortly after this that Doreen asked me if I would conduct some sketching classes on a future cruise. I was very surprised and said I would think about it as Eileen, being an artist too, could also be involved. So we discussed the question of how we would go about it at great length. What preparations would be necessary? Should we organise it as a club? We were invited up to the London office, met members of the staff and taken out to lunch over which we accepted the job – a job that lasted ten years and produced some interesting repercussions. This was at a time when Swan Hellenic was about the only cruise company providing for the interests of artists, art historians and all those searching for information about the classical world. Every cruise had lecturers who spoke informally on sites or in the lecture theatre. The subjects of all lectures were, of course, relevant for the coming visits to museums or ancient sites. Some of which were not easy to find or explore without professional guidance.

This long period was a most interesting time for us especially as there was a break when we were asked to conduct a tour in Provence. We were expected to run this course without any visual material. We were told electrical outlet sockets were very different from those in England which made a projector impossible. Now it just so happened that we were taking a holiday in the area of Avignon so having the address to which we were to take the course, we went along, arrived with the necessary equipment for making a tracing of an outlet socket. This was easily done and on returning to London we assured Swan Hellenic we had the answer to the problem and we would like the projector. We received our equipment but on the condition I carried it which I did, all the way to Avignon! We were in the city during a hot period and the room we used for our lectures had a very low ceiling. The atmosphere got hotter and hotter and it took all our energy keeping everyone awake and attentive.

This was ideal weather for visiting the sites, several of

which we did not know and therefore needed work to be done on them. These working tours were a wonderful opportunity for us, enabling visits to Greek and Roman sites we could never have seen had we been travelling alone. We decided to give the club a name. The *Orpheus* Art Group seemed most appropriate, but this idea needed to be established officially, so we designed a form which we thought would do this. We were inviting takers to say what their main interest was, architecture, plants, landscape, etc. The response was helpful and gave us an indication of how we should prepare. Things were not easy; we had no place in which to work other than in the dining room, but not until it was clear of diners at about 8:45–9:00 AM. Our store was a flight of stairs down so anything we wanted had to be transported up and down each session. But in spite of these problems some good work was done and a unified, small community developed out of a common interest. It was most gratifying to see them helping one another and discussing the work they were doing.

One amusing incident took place when Paul, the Captain, came through the class to see a dustbin lying on its side. He nearly passed out but recovered when we explained it was being used as an exercise in drawing an ellipse. At the beginning of a cruise it was customary to go over our itinerary to let takers know what our aims were. On one such meeting the room was full, over forty-one people, but when the word 'work' came up they vanished leaving us free to concentrate on the serious ones – twelve to fifteen people was just ideal. One year we recruited an exceptional body of enthusiasts which included a mother and daughter, both of whom were very knowledgeable in quite different ways and gave great support. This aid was apparent when we began a project requiring several people to work together. The subject was

'Greek ceramics', the technique being montage with a limited colour scheme. The complete panels, about two foot six inches by one foot six inches, were a surprise to everyone. They were excellent and it was our intention to store them as teaching material for another cruise but the head steward, taking a dislike to us and our work, threw the panels overboard with other materials we were going to use again. It was on one of these cruises we met Freda and Susan Chambers which began a long friendship that took us to America as their guests, ten years running. A most memorable decade.

Our cruising years were most stimulating and rewarding in many ways; 'Cruise 197' being one of them. The itinerary was France, Portugal and Spain in which Eileen and I were both on the list of guest lecturers. It was our first visit to both countries and therefore the customs, costumes, architecture and the people were particularly interesting. We travelled from Barcelona to Alicante in perfect conditions.

We saw for the first time the destructive side of tourism. At the turn of the nineteenth century Alicante must have been a delightful little town judging by the nineteenth-century remnants we saw boarded up, ready for demolition. Our sketching party found just enough existing material to draw by searching, other than the huge unlovely blocks of modern flats and apartments which were growing fast, like mushrooms. We could see nothing attractive in this resort, or quite understand why people flocked there. This was the most barren place we had seen but not, we understand, the only one. Seville had much more to offer our group, not only architecturally but the horse drawn carriages and café life were more interesting for us because a far greater percentage of the citizens were natives to the city. Our sketching party now knew each other and were growing in confidence and enjoyment, to our great satisfaction.

We sailed on to Lagos, then Queluz, in Lisbon, Sintra. Queluz Palace, now unoccupied, had original architectural features created by the architect Robillion in 1782. Oporto had much to offer our students – fascinating boats for transporting wine, a cathedral in which granite was used, its hardness influencing and simplifying the carving. Santiago de Compostela was in no way disappointing – the large square had a variety of architectural styles from the Cathedral's Romanesque portal to late nineteenth century. The hotel, once a private palace, also provided splendid drawing material of which I made use. France gave us rich subject matter. After La Rochelle, Santes Cognac, Aulnay, Surgéres, and back to La Rochelle, this trip provided plenty to digest until Nantes and Angers were left for Brest, Lampant, St Thegonner, St. Malo and Mont St. Michael. My sketch book for August 1981 contains some indication of the kind of cruise we worked on. It provides the Swan pattern for the many journeys we made in Greece, the Greek Islands, The Black Sea, Asia Minor, North Africa and further east to the Spice Islands, Hong Kong and Singapore. Incidentally, after my surgical operation in 1997 we received from Ken Swan a most generous 'get well' card in the form of a three weeks cruise. We thought it was a wonderful gesture.

There were two cruises of special significance for us; the first was the eightieth birthday of the Queen Mother, the second being Prince Charles' first wedding. On these two occasions we arranged to decorate the ship's dining room. For the first one, the Queen Mother's birthday, we made dozens of small shields of the heraldic Bowes-Lyon devices, pinning them to the ceiling. We could not start the work until the dining room was cleared and vacated then standing on tables and chairs went on with the job until 2 AM. We also made a decoration which featured a large photograph of the Queen Mother. This covered a large blackboard on an easel in the main foyer. We went to bed very tired but pleased with the general effect of celebration given by the centrepiece and mobiles. We were not to be satisfied for long because that night we suffered a storm and a rough passage which shattered the main centrepiece. A steward must have found the state of things but instead of replacing it on the easel, put it flat on a dining room table where we found it. An American woman said, 'What a pity that cute picture is not standing up.' So we stood it up! To our great astonishment we saw our cousins from America taking the mobile shields down as souvenirs. We had tried, but were unable to take into consideration the elements of human behaviour. We had better fortune with the decoration celebrating the Royal Wedding. They were all sold, the proceeds going to charity.

One of the lasting things about our experiences on board was the friends we made. Two of our most affectionate are Sir Peter and Lady Sonia Wright. They joined The *Orpheus* Art Group, to talk about some of Sonia's problems working with watercolours. Peter wanted to know how to draw a deck chair in perspective. He told me on a recent visit to see us that he still had my analysis of the problem in the demonstration I made. Peter had a natural talent and during the two weeks he was working with us he produced some very interesting designs influenced by his long association with the Ballet of which he was the Director. Apart from Freda and Susan Chambers, Doreen Goodrick, Margaret and Philip Pearce are people who have enriched our lives. Doreen in particular because she has been patron and support from the beginning. I know of no other storyteller quite equal to Doreen's fluent, humorous and descriptive power. We have often said what a pity she is not speaking into a recording machine, they would make such wonderful reading. Doreen was also an excellent cruise director. I think it was Margaret who boasted that she was the only person who had swam through the Corinthian Canal – in the swimming pool! Margaret is also an historian and is a guide for Hampton Palace. Philip is a well-read, humorous and affectionate friend. He and Margaret once worked for British Air – they now make the most of their flying concessions as you would expect. Cards came from every corner of the globe. Our most respected friends are Marion and Kenneth Swan. One evening the captain's table was short of two guests. Eileen and I were with a group at a nearby table when the head steward came across to us and said, 'You are summoned to the captain's table'. I looked up and said, 'Is this an order?' and he said, 'Yes'. I think this was the action that cemented our friendship. Kenneth and Marion were not on every cruise, of course, but it was not the same without them. They graced the special occasions when gentlemen wore dinner jackets and the ladies appeared in feminine splendour. There is much to be said for recognising, and dressing for, a special event.

These cruises provided many memorable incidents which enriched the day. The sight of a shoal of dolphins feeding in their dozens was one of these. The event was so rare that the captain turned the ship round – we returned back a few miles through the Arabian Sea to enable us to have a prolonged viewing of these animals, something you only do easily in a small ship. These delightful creatures have always captivated artists of the past particularly in Greece and Rome.

Of the considerable number of interesting historical sites we have visited in Greece, Asia Minor and North Africa, some have provided information of exceptional importance to an understanding of past civilisations. Of these, Priene in Turkey is one. Its remaining underground lavatory system is remarkably complete in spite of the vandalism of peoples and time. It indicates what a civilised prosperous city it must have been, providing public facilities over two thousand years before anything comparable was available in Europe.

Pergamon, however, is situated on a hillside spur overlooking an extensive panoramic view of miles of verdant fields and woods, a view which must have delighted the audiences being entertained in the theatre, built into the hillside. On entering the enclosed site a stylobate on the left is all that remains of a great altar to Zeus. It is renowned for the sides which were decorated in deep relief sculpture by Scopas depicting the wards between Gods and giants. These large panels were the first examples of the emotionalism inherent in the Pergamon School which flourished in 180–150 BC. The slabs were removed by the Germans and are now in Berlin. Scopas worked on the Mausoleum at Halicarnassus (now known as Bodrum in Turkey) for Mausolus and his wife Artemisia. The colossal statues of these two in the British Museum would seem to be by Scopas since they feature all the characteristics of his work.

Enclosed in its site, Ephesus contains very considerable remains of what was once a great city. There are sufficient remains of buildings still standing to give a clear picture of what life would have been like in Hellenistic times. In particular, the library has been restored from all the original excavated materials presenting a very impressive building of three stories with the honey coloured stone shining in the sunshine. The cobbled and paved streets include curb stones carved with the impression of a shoe pointing the way to the establishments where short-term company could be had for a fee! On one of these streets was situated the public lavatories with running water as an expression of wealth, ease and luxury. In addition to the library, a number of small, commemorative temples, of which Trojan's was a good example, still enrich the site.

The town of Nazareth was quite a different matter. Dirty streets and litter gave the impression of neglect. Nothing was sacrosanct; there was no feeling that there was anything special or holy about the place. The main purpose of our visit was to see the Church of the Nativity. My reaction was one of complete disillusionment. There was little to recommend its outside aspect and the inside was rather awful. In fact, it was hideous because of the large decorations which covered the walls donated, presumably, by Christian countries, which seemed to have been competing with one another. The result was a brash, disturbing confusion. Whoever was in charge of the project, a committee of some sort I imagine, should have emphasised the need for artists to conform to one colour scheme as a means of harmonising an uninteresting interior. I thought of other venerable monuments – the Parthenon, St. Sophia, St. Peter's in Rome – but the Church of the Nativity could not be added to these places of worship with much confidence.

Unfortunately, the *Minerva* (the successor to the *Orpheus*) did not please everyone, like the pair who said they were getting off at the next port. They were on the wrong cruise – no leg shows, no chorus girls, no jazz bands. The Hellenic cruise was not for them! They should have been on the *Queen Elizabeth II* when we crossed the Atlantic homeward bound from one of our journeys to America. The food consumed was phenomenal but the most disturbing behaviour was at the midnight buffet when some men appeared in their singlet vests and paper party hats, a far cry from the conduct of the first *QEII* passengers.

The banquet prepared by professional cooks was sumptuous. There were large joints of every sort and attractively presented dishes of every kind were being attacked by what would seem to be a starved and deprived society.

One other example will suffice. We helped a pair of publicans who had been given the prize of a cruise as a present. They were completely out of their depth, poor things. They sat at our allocated table throughout the journey which was embarrassing for them as they could not even cope with the menu. Such experiences threw light on the state of society and the unique position Swan Hellenic held, but for how long? Times are changing rapidly; there has been acceleration in the numbers of cruisers who are not travelling to increase the knowledge of their passengers of other peoples and their cultures, but for pleasure only. Let us hope Swan Hellenic continues to remain true to its original purpose.

Swan Hellenic and America

One morning in our correspondence was a letter from Freda inviting us to visit them in Tucson, Arizona, but having had this kind of invitation before we politely turned it down. However, quite shortly afterwards came another more pressing proposal that we might reconsider our decision and come for two weeks. We had never been to America. The idea of going to the USA had never crossed our minds. We wondered whether we should accept and go, and that is what we did. Our knowledge of this continent was very meagre. We went to find out where Arizona was.

The first flight gave us a clear picture of the size, the huge size of this land mass. It was as far to Tucson from the East Coast as it was from London to New York. We were met at the small aerodrome of Tucson by Freda who drove us to Camino Antonio. We understood that the Chambers lived in the desert but their twenty-five acres were much more than sand! The Chambers' estate was covered in semi-tropical shrubs, small trees and the strange cactus saquira which can grow fifteen to twenty feet tall and weigh tons when swollen after rain. Another, the night blooming cactus, only grows in Arizona where it can present a most impressive sight when seen on hill and mountain slopes growing in large numbers to a height of twenty to thirty feet. When travelling from one state to another it gradually fades out giving place to entirely different vegetation. This cactus, after seven or eight years, grows arms which first appear as small knobs on the trunk. After rainfall the plant can weigh up to seven tons. The blooms on the top of the main stem resemble a coronet of white flowers, the seeds from which were once eaten by the native Indians. When the plant dies and the outside rots away it leaves a skeleton, consisting of a number of long narrow ribs which provide material for ceilings giving a most pleasing decorative result.

On our first visit to Freda's house we were given the guest house – a completely equipped building adjacent to the main large bungalow complex. The first visit was experimental. Freda, I am sure, wanted to know what our reactions were. I remember her walking across the large parking area with a bottle of whiskey for us as a symbol of her welcome and hospitality. This was the only time we ever used the guest house. From then on we were given a commodious bedroom in the main building with Union Jack pillow cases and a large window overlooking the Catalina Mountains. We used this room on our visits for another nine years.

Freda's daughter, Susan, was a very gifted woman who

graduated in Japan but sadly, for some unknown reason, developed the illness anorexia. During the twelve years we knew her she got thinner and thinner with the compulsion to walk miles, sometimes reading at the same time. She walked alone, unless giving the dog exercise. This need must have used up what little nourishment the scrap of food she ate produced. Susan had a captivating sense of humour. One of our long drives, this time from Phoenix we suddenly looked round from our front seats to see Susan wearing a huge Mexican moustache. The Chambers were great entertainers. Susan was continually cooking or preparing food for supper for as many as sixteen. It was after one of these gatherings that Kim, our great friend and professional pianist would give a concert to a much enlarged number than the supper party.

Two great friends of Freda's were John and Martha Riley. They always formed part of any party or concert being given at Camino Antonio. I painted a portrait of Freda but when Wid was clearing the house prior to selling it he said he did not want it, but John and Martha did. So it is now with the best friends. If Freda had knowledge of this I am sure it would have given her great pleasure but also grief to think that her son did not want it.

It was to this intimate audience that my talks were given on diverse subjects which included 'Kentish Hall House', The 'Coopers' wall decorations, etc. We thought this was the best way to repay something for their continued generous hospitality. It was after my talk on the 'Kentish Hall House' that John said, 'I'm very surprised to hear you once lived in a "whore's" house'. Pause . . . laughter.

Freda booked a hotel on the Mexican seaboard because she thought we should know something of this neighbour state. We were taken to the Grand Canyon, and as we approached

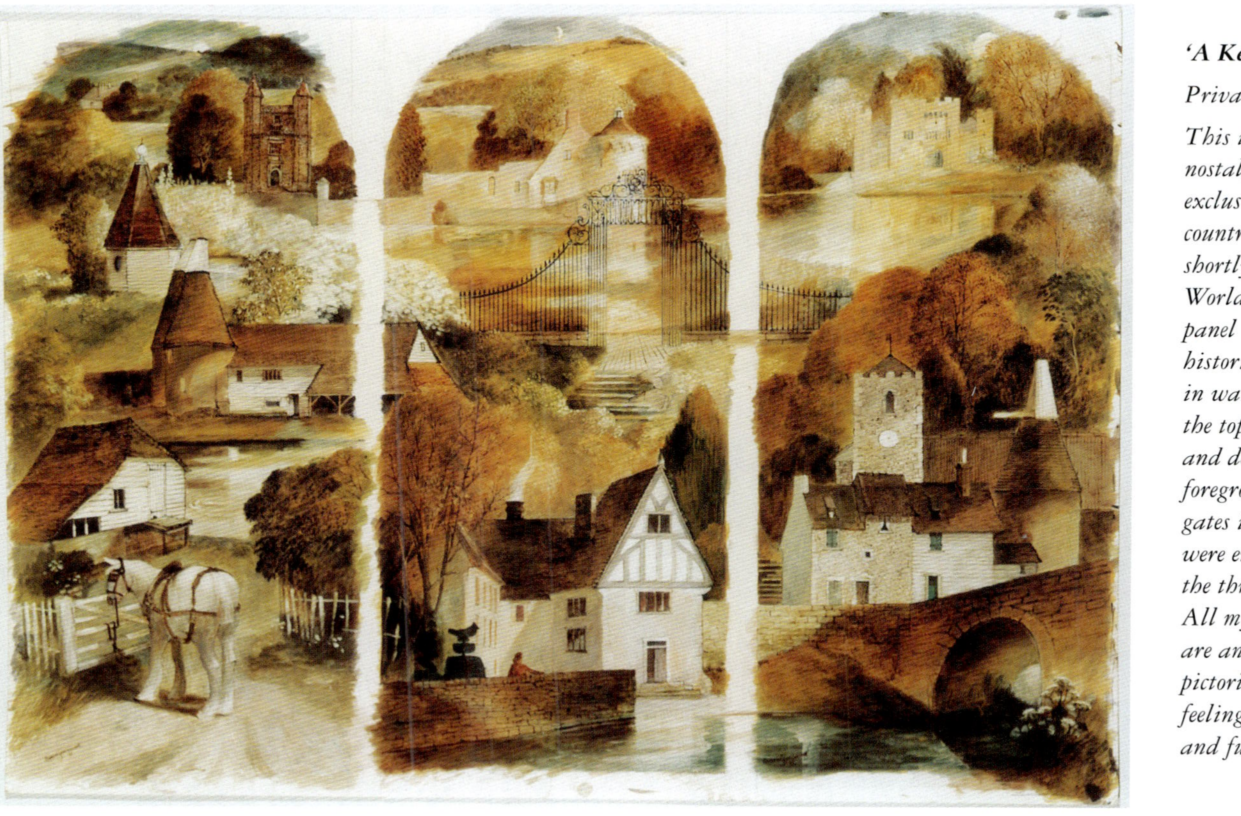

'A Kentish idyll'

Private Collection.

This unapologetically nostalgic painting is based exclusively on the Kent countryside as it was shortly after the Second World War. On top of each panel there is a Kent historic building reflected in water which flows from the top to middle distance and down into the foreground. The decorative gates in the centre panel were employed to help bring the three panels together. All my paintings of Kent are an effort to find a pictorial equivalent of my feelings about present, past and future.

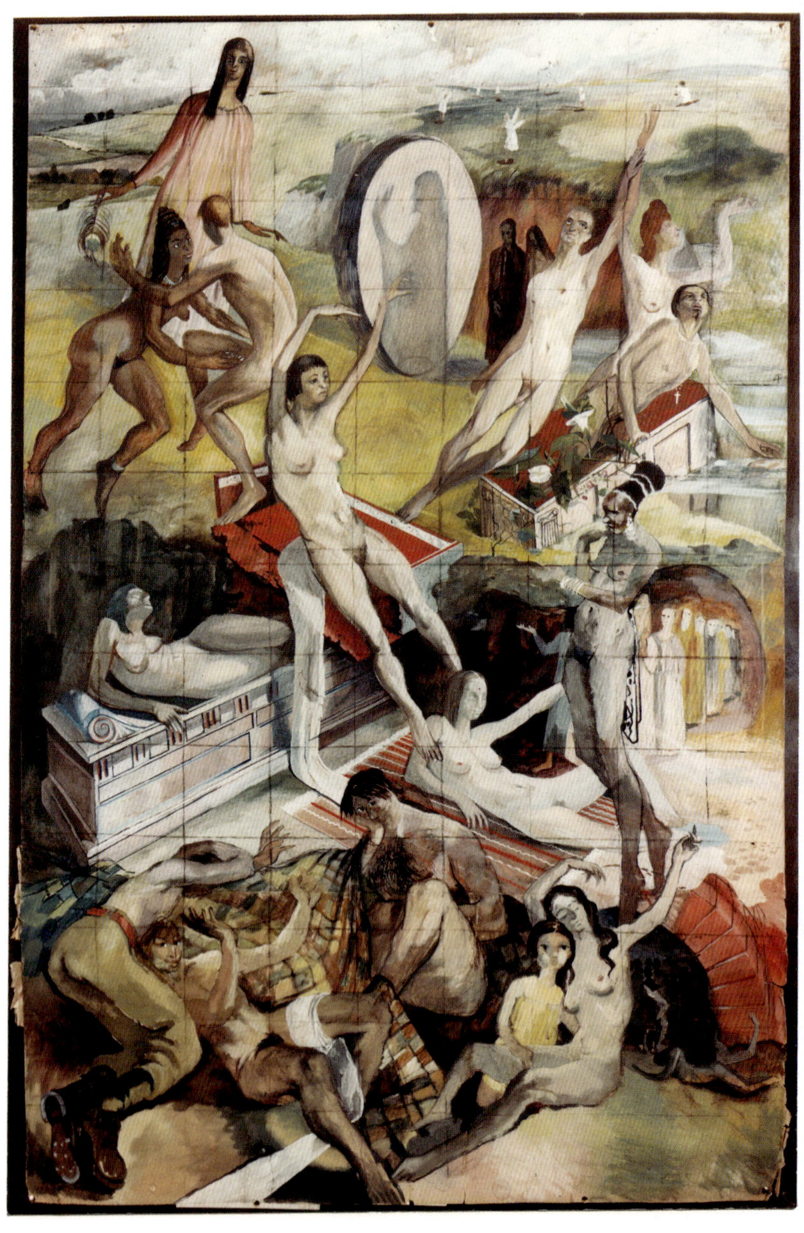

'Resurrection 1'

Gouache on paper. 1943. The original design for an oil painting ready and squared for transfer to the canvas.

Painted during the sunny days of autumn on the back of what had been an itinerant preacher's horse-drawn caravan situated in the grounds of Wilton Park. The influence of this environment dictated the colour and treatment of the subject.

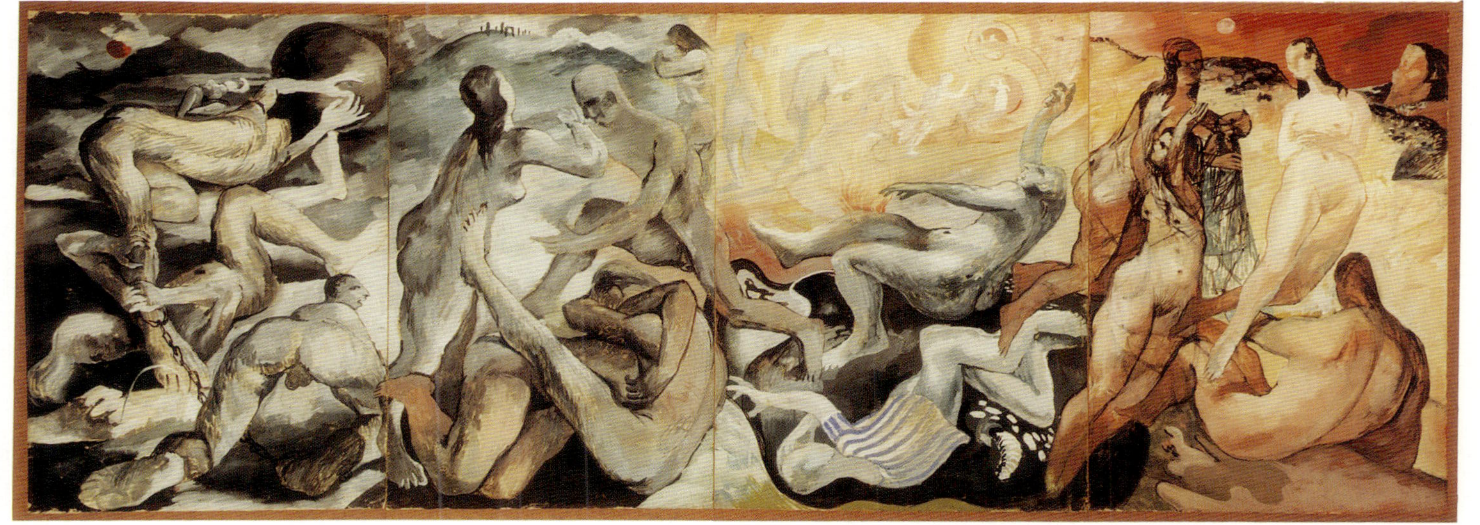

'Resurrection 2'

Painted in Berlin in response to the horrors experienced by prisoners of the Nazi prison camps. This dictated an entirely different approach to the subject in which a certain lyrical attitude in the first Resurrection is in contrast to a visual representation of the atrocities of genocide. The two are placed side by side to help illustrate the fundamentally disparate responses to human life.

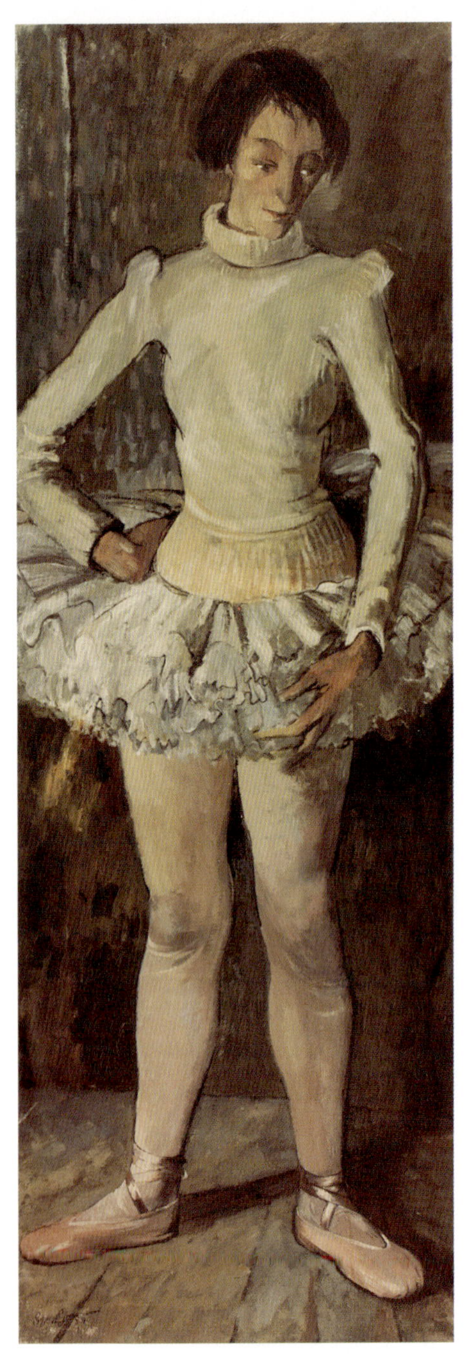

'The Dancer'

My only full length portrait; this is the first of many I thought I might produce but circumstances did not permit this.

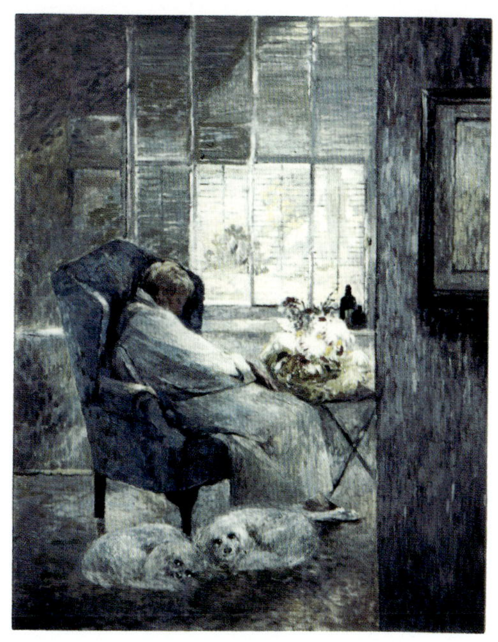

'Freda resting with Windy and Suggy'

Oil. 1995. Private Collection. Arizona U.S.A. Freda's last days.

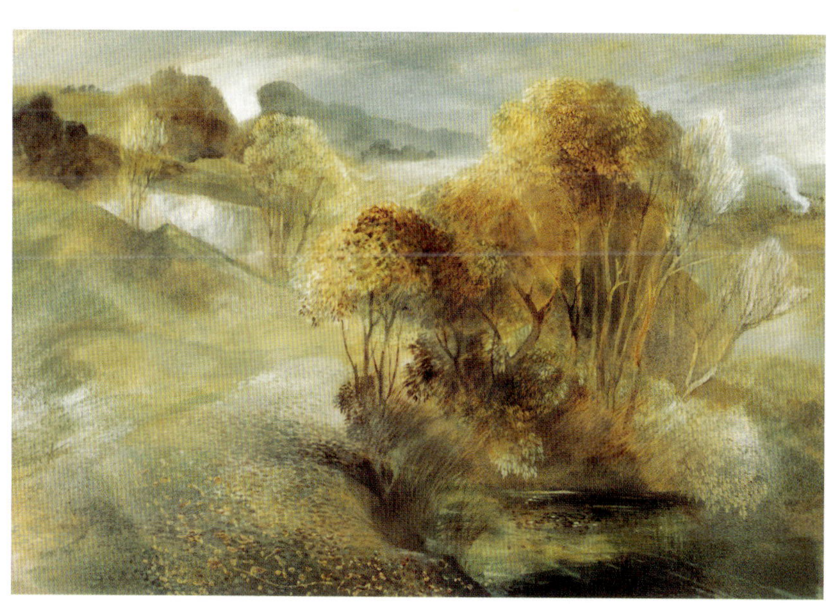

Watercolour of North Downs

A disused quarry on the Downs.

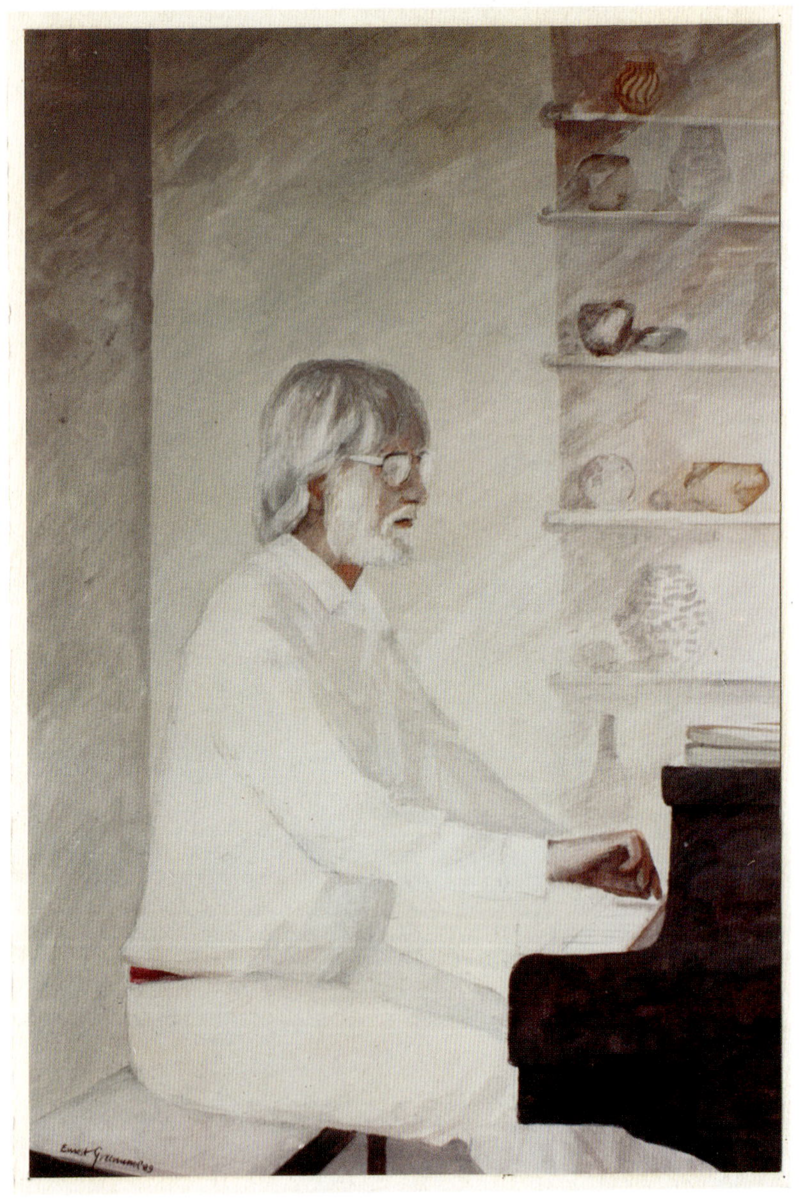

'Dan plays Haydn'

Watercolour. 1989. Private Collection. U.S.A.

Dan is dedicated to the study and collection of works of art. He is a great friend with whom we shared many concerts and recitals.

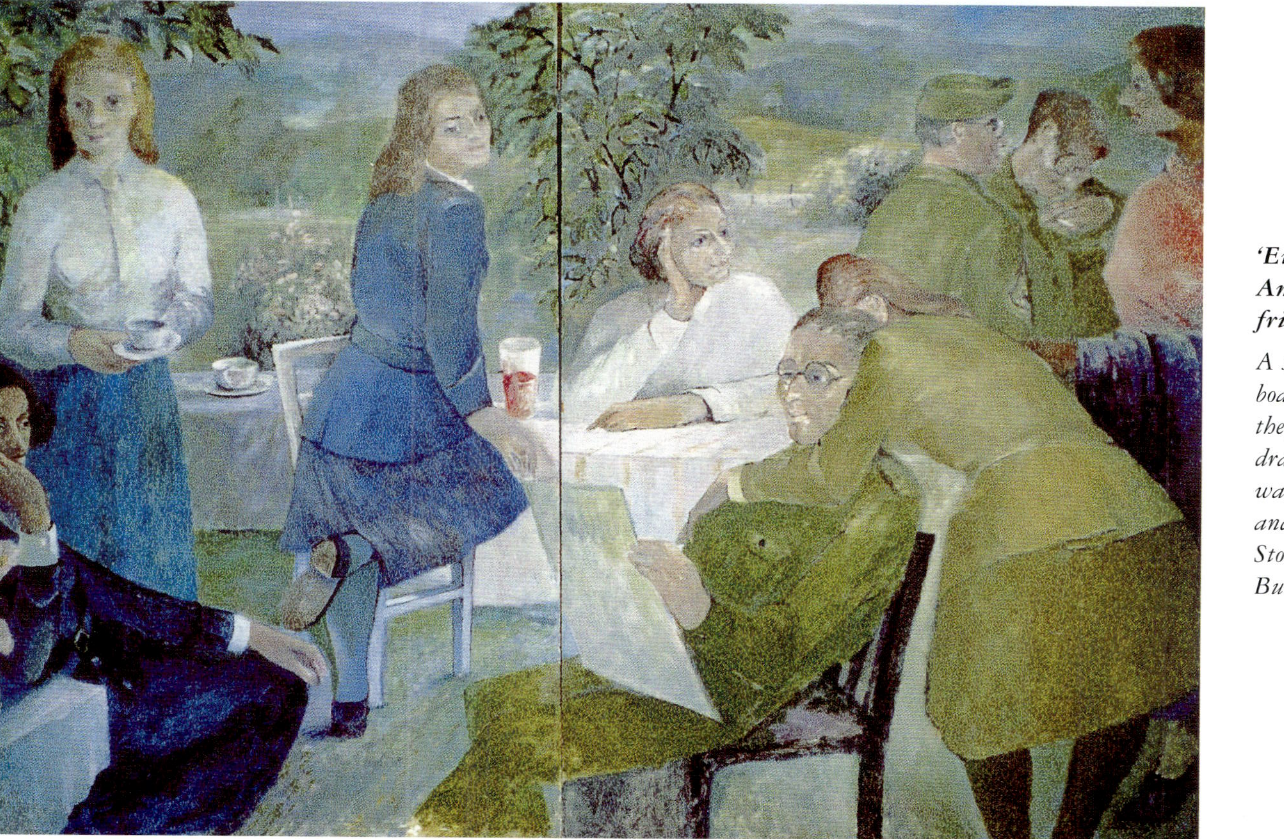

'English and American friends'

A sketch in oil on board made from the full size drawing (pencil on wash) now framed and glazed in the Stocks Gallery in Bungay.

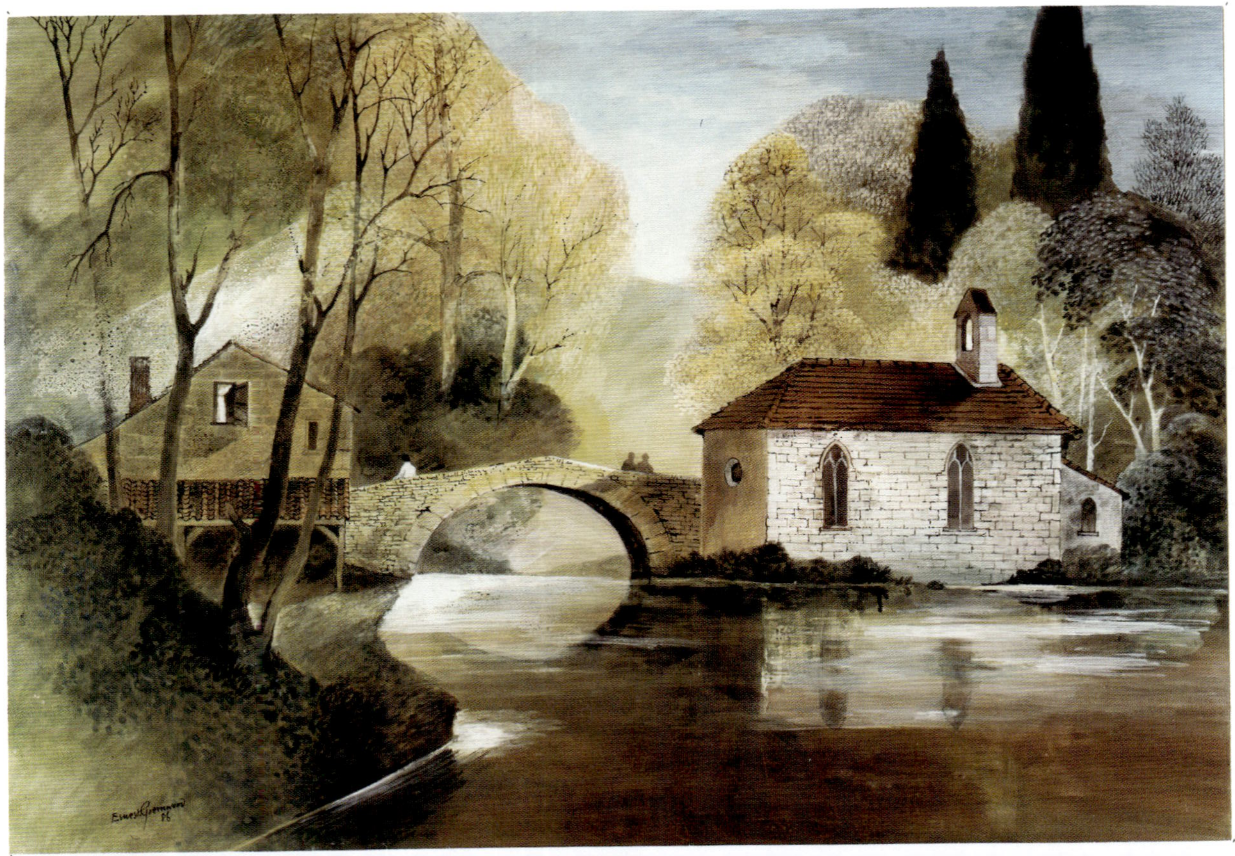

'The Chapel for the Lock Keepers'

Watercolour. 1986. Private Collection.

A chapel on the Canal du Midi.

the edge, Debbie, Susan's friend said, 'Close your eyes.' then a few steps on said, 'Now open your eyes.', so that I found myself gazing down into this awe-inspiring canyon. A number of artists have attempted to use this remarkable phenomenon as subject matter for paintings but few have succeeded. Energetic walkers have gone down to the Colorado River to explore its course to the sea. This river is being drained to supply water to the rapidly growing gambling complex of Las Vegas in the desert – without a natural supply of water of any kind. Our short visit of three days was a revelation. It is huge; a colossal fun fair of outrageous proportions designed to attract, like a magnet, the millions of visitors who flock to the gambling booths. It is equipped with row upon row of machines by the thousands in which men and women sit, of every nationality, hour by hour, obtaining the necessary change from scantily dressed females. The buildings are quite enormous, if you can so call some of the creations which are copies of great classical monuments. For example, the Great Pyramid of Giza, almost actual size, in glass, with the Nile running though it and boats to take you on a mystery tour. It is, in fact, just one of the many hotels to provide accommodation for the international masses who come to gaze and in many cases, leave their money too. This is the Disney World plus – but many times, with a sinister ubiquity which is lost in the pleasure of suppressed excitement.

Susan had to be working for her size and physique prodigiously. She painted flowers, plants and vegetables in watercolours, some of which were simplified into patterns for her silk screen printing at which she laboured diligently, producing garments for children and adults. This frantic activity seemed to be associated with her illness. On every one of our internal flights, of which there were many, Susan would be writing her letters on what ever came to hand. We received letters of this kind very frequently in England. In spite of this aspect of her character she had a personal appreciation of innumerable things, especially the good qualities in other people. Susan cultivated people who were associated with many different organisations and professions. She supported children's welfare, wild life, women's crafts, botanical gardens and individuals in need of support. A special friend was Kim Hyashi, a pianist who has achieved great success as a concert performer in America and Europe. To Kim we have become much attached. He calls us every two or three weeks and sends us copies of his recitals, the most recent being a concert in memory of Freda Chambers. I made an oil painting on board from a drawing I made of him during one of his concerts. I sent it through the post and it arrived safely.

I never heard Susan criticise anybody. All of her friends treated her with affectionate generosity. The thing she needed most was intimate affection which she achieved on her marriage to Art, a widower whom we knew. His first wife died from an occupationary disease. This marriage to Art was altruistic in so far as it was entirely done out of a sympathetic knowledge of the conditions prevailing. Freda was very ill and required constant attention with which Art coped. In one essential, but non-emotional way he also looked after Susan. He did much more for these two women than ever the son, Wid, considered doing. He, by contrast, took himself off and lived miles away, and having plenty of money this was not difficult. Art and Susan paid us a visit in 1998. Susan was unwell on the flight and on arriving at Brushings Farmhouse went to bed. Their visit to us was cut short. We ordered a taxi and they left for Heathrow with Susan looking very ill. Freda had died and it looked as if Susan had a very brief future.

Debbie, her intimate friend, had warned Susan that unless she ate and put on some weight, she would be unable to battle with an illness. Time proved how right she was, Susan died only a few months after she left us. Art was doing his last kindness when he had the life support machine switched off. Had Susan lived through this crisis she would have been an invalid, unable to walk or enjoy her much loved square dancing. Freda, a competent landscape painter, and Susan, were two remarkable women. Freda was so generous, financing most of our journeys to Salt Lake City, Monument Valley, Phoenix (where we stayed in a luxurious hotel in order to visit the Frank Lloyd Wright Architectural School, now looking very shabby), Seattle, Texas and so many other expeditions. We had at least one major journey each year.

In 1997 we were in Philadelphia staying with Freda's sister. The same summer we witnessed the extraordinary festival of St. Xavier. The Abbey Church was only a few miles from Tucson which we reached after a short drive. The festival originated in the seventeenth century adoration of the Virgin Mary, a catholic cult imported into Mexico from Spain. A chain of these mission churches once spread from Mexico to Tucson. St. Xavier is the best preserved, although one or two are still in use, others are in a sad state of dilapidation disguised by a brash use of paint. The festival in which we participated that evening was quite a dramatic, entertaining event, reminiscent of our bonfire night. A small hillock nearby was illuminated by a huge head of the Virgin from which a long avenue of two rows of bonfires ran in a straight line to the Church and, as my drawing records, were met there by a host of men carrying large banners. The crowds were immense. The food booths were busy selling the traditional fare similar to our pancakes. It was quite spectacular, having something of a pagan ritual about it. Clearing up the litter the next morning must have been a major task.

Dan Leach was a frequent member of the luncheon parties that Susan and Freda gave, as were Daniel and Ray. These were but three of the many friends made during these ten years in America. Dan is an art collector, a very cultivated and wealthy bachelor who has travelled extensively in Europe. He made a special trip to Maidstone to see my last exhibition and bought a large watercolour to join his other four Greenwoods in Tucson. David and Ray invited us to an evening out to dine at a very special steak house before leaving Camino Antonio. Ray said, 'Don't wear a special tie, it won't be seen anyway', but gave us no reason for the remark. I found out later! We were taken to a steak house with a real 'western' flavour – a smoky, dim atmosphere, where the many beams hung with hundreds of neck ties. Steaks of two sizes were served – a 'cowboy' and 'cowgirl', each one large enough to provide protein for a week at least. Just before being served a western cowgirl arrived with an enormous pair of scissors and cut through my tie just under the knot. It was about to join all the others decorating the beams where I imagine it still hangs. I am so pleased I did not wear anything special, but it was entertaining!

Another unique event took place when we were asked to contribute to an exhibition of work by a husband and wife in a gallery somewhere (in the back of beyond) near Tucson. We dispatched paintings and prints which arrived safely and we had the pleasure of exhibiting with American artists.

Susan's brother, Wid, was tall with thin, long hair. He was a personality with whom we made no contact. He never did a thing for anyone. He made his own coffee in Susan's kitchen, leaving her to clear up his mess, took his coffee down to the guest house which he had taken over and let no one in, not even his sister. He too had money, as Freda told me, and was happy to live a thousand miles from Tucson. He bought a large studio miles from his house in the woods where he lived alone. It was Wid who inherited the valuable property on Freda's and Susan's death – an estate in which he had no love or interest. Art, having married Susan, was now Wid's brother-in-law, having some claim on the estate. The twenty-five acres was a fortune with developers anxious to get their hands on it. This happened in 2004 when Wid sold out. It is sad to realise that Camino Antonio is no more. It is now raised to the ground – a decade of life filled with so much enjoyment, friendship, generosity and achievement has gone, leaving no trace of its past.

On one of our visits to Tucson, Freda arranged for us to call on her sister living in Philadelphia. This part of our journey we did by train. On arriving at the station and stepping on to the platform a very polite American gentleman insisted on carrying our bags up the steps and on to the road where Freda's sister awaited us in her car. She lived in a high class suburb of the city with lots of mature trees in the immediate vicinity. Our short stay was delightful as were the two dogs she lived with. As with most American cities it was clean and spacious but had no outstanding architecture. The museum was the exception which, like most American collections, contained a number of European works of outstanding quality. The building stands on a wide flight of steps overlooking the city. It has a special transport system designed to transport visitors to places of particular interest, one of which was the house where, in 1776, Betsy Ross is reputed to have made the first stars and stripes flag which has become the national emblem and had been used ever since.

We were introduced to a delightful married woman living

in Boston by a school friend. When we received an invitation to pay a visit we decided to break our journey to the west and spend a night or two in Boston. Escorted by our new friend we found the city of great interest associated as it was with the Boston Tea Party and England. Places of particular interest for the visitor were indicated by a line of red bricks let into the pavement thereby making a local map unnecessary – rather like Ariadne finding her way through the labyrinth by means of letting out a cord. The art gallery was another American collection that was well represented by small paintings by Monet, but Boston had too many which we thought were not all genuine. However, we enjoyed the contents of the gallery, the city and our stay. At home we tend to thing of a city as being a civic development around a castle and cathedral. I am not sure how you designate a city in America unless by its size!

We were quite amazed when visiting the Gardner collection in Boston. It was like entering through a gate in the curtain wall of a fortress. The contents of the house took some time to sort out which, well, like many, many others, have never managed to disentangle the haphazard way in which thousands of objects, large and small, cover the walls, landings and stairs in a profusion of unrelated exhibits. A very great painting by Titian, a product of his later years, was hung so high and surrounded by so many small objects that the work was difficult to enjoy. This masterpiece, 'The Rape of Europa', is one of a group of seven paintings based loosely on Ovid's 'Metamorphoses', but each one can stand alone as a great work of art. 'The Rape of Europa' once graced the walls of Lord Darnley's home 'Cobham Hall'. At a time of financial pressure, Burckhardt, a Swiss historian of the nineteenth century bought it for a mere pittance for the Gardner collection where it now hangs ignominiously, seen by few. We took a taxi driven by an African man who wore no shoes or socks but whose politeness was second to none.

One morning, back in England, I had a letter from an American friend which contained a cheque. I took the cheque to our local Natwest branch but the clerk, doubting its authenticity, looked up, expressing grave concern and saying that he could not cash the cheque, but advised me to take it to one of their London branches and gave me an address. So up to London I went, to the underground nearest to the address. I emerged only to find waiting to cross the road made difficult because of the protecting boarding covering a huge rebuilding development which covered the pavement. I eventually crossed by hugging the fencing for safety and proceeded on my way. I seemed to walk miles in search of a Natwest sign but, at last, one came into sight, so I walked in feeling I had succeeded. I was ushered into an expensive looking armchair and asked to wait. In time I was beckoned to the cashier and handed over the suspect cheque. After some suspense with extreme gravity he said, 'I'm sorry Sir but this is the wrong branch. You must take this cheque to the main bank down the street'. He then pointed back the way I had come. So off I went for another long walk until at last there was the 'Mecca', on the other side of the road, necessitating another hazardous crossing which was safely negotiated with those helpful traffic lights. I entered through glass doors into a great reception area occupied by a single man at a large desk with a worried expression, rather like Atlas carrying the world on his shoulders. But he did rouse himself enough to tell me this was not the bank, but instead it was 'over there'. He told me to go through those glass doors, down the steps, being careful as they are rather steep, turn right along the path, then down more steps onto a narrow service road, walk to the end and then up the steps into the main building. By this time my feet were feeling the effect of so much hard pavement. 'Sit down, Sir. Would you mind waiting?' I dropped once more into an expensive arm-chair and began another long wait until a young woman beckoned me over to her patch of counter. I handed in my cheque, which was handed to a senior who disappeared into the manager's room. After some time the manager himself came out of his *inner sanctum* and looked me over to see if there was any dandruff on my jacket (these were the jacket-wearing days!). He looked me up and down then asked me to sit down and wait – something I was getting rather good at! Eventually he emerged from his room all smiles and said, 'Mr. Greenwood, it's not what you know but who you know that matters'. Handing me the cash for my cheque, I thought how right he was!

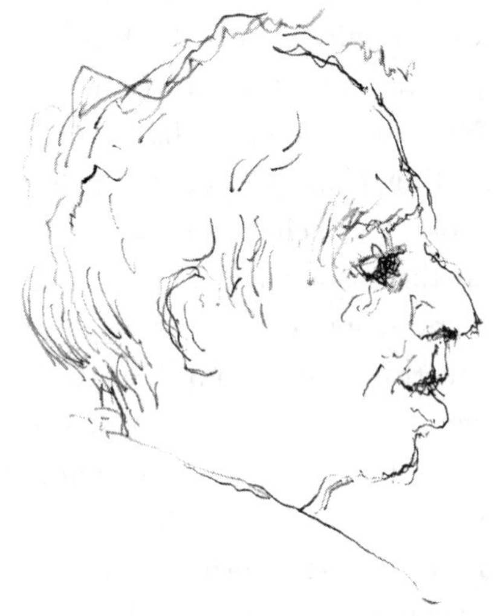

Swan Hellenic and India

Our two journeys to India with Swan Hellenic were two of our most memorable. These tours were instructive in so many ways, particularly in the matter of the Raj and the hundred years of British rule. It is fashionable today to be deprecating, to be contemptuous and self-condemnatory of British influence and work in India which our personal experience has helped to modify.

The period of the British Raj was dominated by our national confidence and competence by the installation of railway stations, in the fields of engineering with bridges and road construction, in medicine, education and politics, even the Indian Parliament is based on our Westminster. All these essential services were introduced by us to a nation in urgent need and has since profited thereby. However, the period of British rules was not free from aspects of domination with actions that were not to our credit.

Our first journey recalled the main problem – population. The sub-continent of India has 59 dialects, spoken over a number of countries and islands. Further east, Vietnam, Cambodia, Borneo, Thailand and the Spice Islands . . . To all thinking people this must be most troubling especially when trying to establish social services and health care. The drive from Bombay airport to our hotel took us through a honeycomb of slum dwellings, hundreds maybe thousands of one-room shelters constructed with any and every type of waste material that could be found, but with no water, no sanitation, no lighting or cooking needs. These are, or were (I would like to think they are now in the past) the conditions in which an innumerable number of people existed. There are so many unwanted children, as we saw in Bombay where a child had been left on the pavement. Seeing this Meem said, 'Surely someone will pick up this doomed mite', but observing, among the teeming mass of people, a boy with a performing bear, I replied, 'That bear is more important than the child, it is earning their suppers'.

Hinduism is the religion of the vast majority (about eighty per cent) of the people of India. There was no one founder, no

Bible, no Pope, but a slow development over a long period of time in which many schools of Hinduism have grown up without a static Sanskrit, although Brahma is the core deity, being the creator of the universe, the impersonal eternal and absolute principle. It is abundant in mythology and practices. Indian epics, longer than the *Iliad* or *Odyssey*, were written down about 400 BC, but infused with superstition, as with most religions, is an unfounded fear, an ignorant and irrational conviction of a supernatural agency. This belief is having a powerful influence, creating fanatics, as we saw on our way down a long flight of steps leading to the Ganges at Banares. At the top stood a money changer who converted Rupees into small units for distribution to the holy men sitting in cages. There was one man who had been holding one arm up so long it had petrified, and the uncut nails had grown into talons. On the river bank a flat platform used for cremation purposes was in use, the end results being thrown into the river where scores of people of all ages were bathing. Can emancipation ever free these believers from all the self-inflicted tortures they suffer for no purpose?

My drawing of a Jain temple prompted me to investigate the differences between the three main practices: Hinduism, Jainism and Buddhism. The last two resulted from a revolt from the Hindu caste system supported by the poor people. Jainism was founded about 500 BC in Western Bengal and was opposed to the killing of anything. This has resulted in most adherents becoming money-lenders, financiers and tradesmen. Buddhism – Buddha meaning the enlightened one – is taught through conversations, parables and stories. Disciples went from town to town meditating in the day, discoursing at night. This philosophy was spread by monks to Sri Lanka, north east of China, Japan, Korea and the whole of southeast Asia. After

Buddha's death Buddhism went through two thousand years of transition in which splinter groups established themselves. Jainism and Buddhism have much in common, they became a serious challenge to Brahma orthodoxy.

India and countries in the Far East have all produced monuments in works of art and architecture of great power and interest. They all required concentrated study which I would like to have given to those I was fortunate to see.

From Bombay we travelled north to Delhi and the area rich in the works of the Mogul occupation. The Taj Mahal in Agra is in every way unique. Its proportions seen in silhouette show

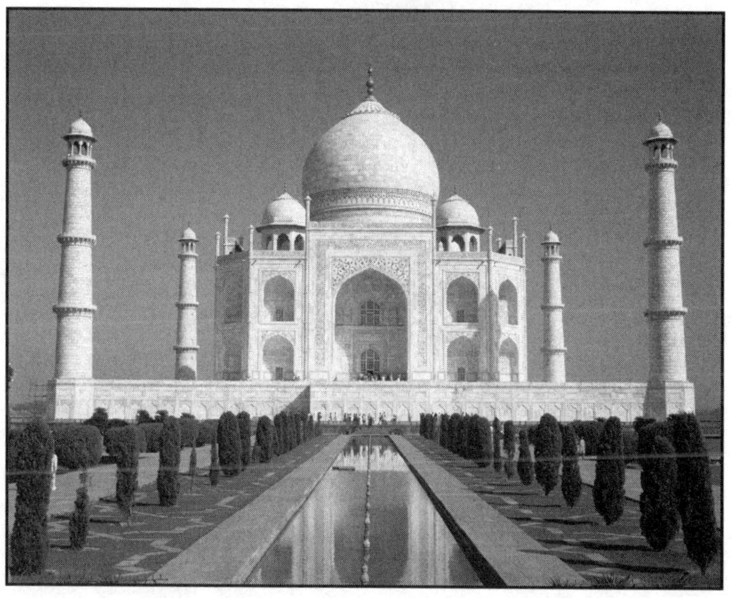

quite clearly the care with which the architect designed the relationship between the masses. These proportions are controlled mathematically and geometrically. For example, the total height of the magnificent dome is exactly half the total

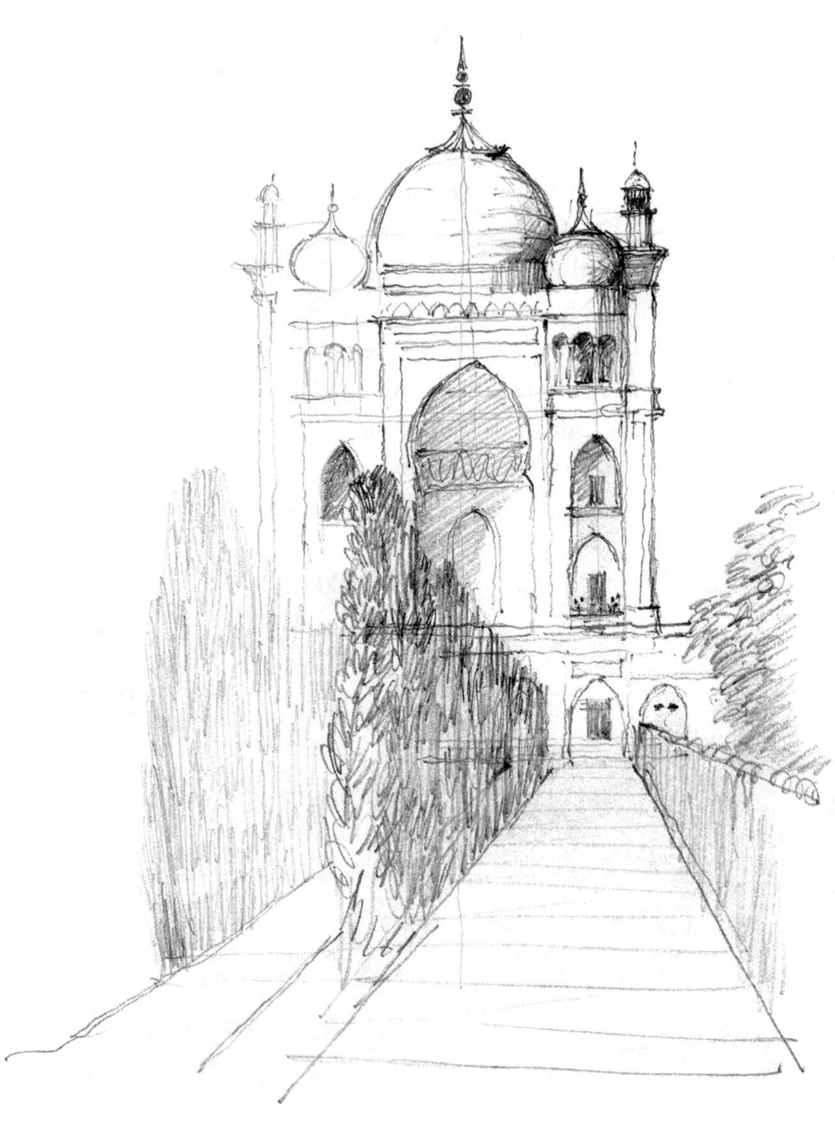

Tomb of Empress Daurami by Aurangzeb

height of the building and half the width producing a complete square into which all the other parts are related. These principles of design are similar to those used by Ictinus and the contractor Calicrates when they designed the Parthenon. Forty years after the Taj was completed his son, Aurangzeb, had built a mausoleum to house the tomb of the Empress Daurami. The same elements were used, but what a difference in the result. The different parts of the building have all been squeezed together with an unsatisfactory visual result. The dome looks as though it is falling into a void, the front elevation having too many open spaces, giving a sense of insecurity to the whole structure. It also lacks the spaciousness of the Taj, as this building is hemmed in by avenues of trimmed trees.

The Taj Mahal and its Persian water garden are a splendid creation but the Lake Palace is wonderful. It is built mostly of white marble in a valley later dammed up to form a large lake with the palace in the centre. The visual result in an evening light is quite dreamlike and poetic. Its ethereal impact could never be expressed in graphic terms; like the Taj and so many other concepts as Ankar Wat in Cambodia where water plays an important part in imposing an awareness of the existence of eternal verities. The water surrounding many great temples has now dried up. Those imposing buildings singly, or in groups, must have employed thousands of labourers and craftsmen of the highest order, particularly the sculptors, all working under the direction of a great architect. Such projects could only be achieved by one man amassing fabulous wealth, which was used solely to realise one man's worship and veneration of the gods, coupled with the builder's magnificence. The Moguls built many splendid forts and palaces with a strong Moorish influence in their decoration, especially prominent in windows and doors.

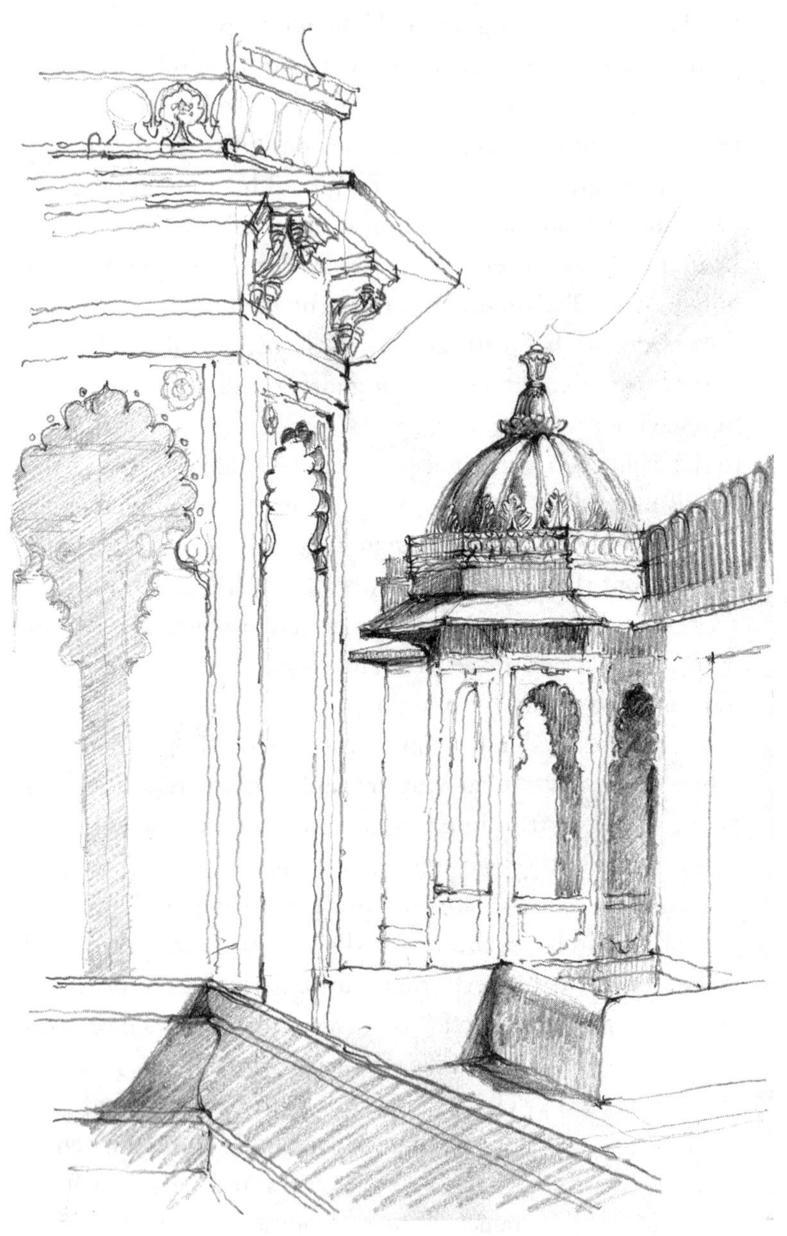

Lake Palace architectural decoration

Since its independence in 1947, the population of India has risen from three hundred and fifty million to one billion in about fifty years. India has become a unified democratic country with a free articulate press and a middle class equal to the population of the USA. India has become a powerhouse, opening up to the rest of the world with Vietnam and Thailand moving in the same direction.

* * *

Great architectural achievements might have been possible in Britain if there had been a need for more than a millennium dome! But we have plenty of cash accumulated to pay for a phoney war with an army hunting for a non-existent bomb and to build football stadia which resemble the Roman Circus in appearance and function both built to entertain the thousands who patronise the game. Juvenal made the cryptic comment when he said, 'The only two things people anxiously desire are bread and the circus'. One could paraphrase this statement by saying, yes football and chips, the BBC to supply the football, McDonalds the chips. But snooker has emerged for those people who find great enjoyment watching two contestants match their skills against each other. From its inception in 1875 the word 'snooker' probably derived from an old military slang word and since television began broadcasting the sport, the game had become an internationally competitive institution and for a few top players a very lucrative profession. Like cricket, the game has now spread all over the world. But the difference in terms of prize money should be more fairly adjusted. No cricketer to my knowledge has ever won two hundred and fifty thousand pounds!

VIII
THE CANAL VENTURES

TWO OF OUR MOST MEMORABLE JOURNEYS were on the French Canal du Midi. The first with Grace, who went to the same school as Eileen, Camden School for Girls, (but a few years earlier), and her husband Digby. They were not at all adventuresome and we carried them both. Grace contracted a back complaint necessitating medical advice. I cannot recall how this was obtained, but the work or course, fell on Eileen. This meant regular injections into a particular part of the spine, the spot being marked with a circle. It was of course, done well, and Grace recovered, but it was not the best of holiday activities. Nevertheless, we thought it was a great way to travel into the countryside at walking speed as it enabled us to see and observe a great deal. It was also a splendid way to draw and take notes. I made a number of these studies which provided material for the subject matter in my collection of paintings of France. The evening and night time were the most restful. It was then, under the stars with a clear, warm, unpolluted atmosphere, that the wildlife became active, producing a movement in an otherwise mirror-like water. The smell alone made a wonderful restorative, it was

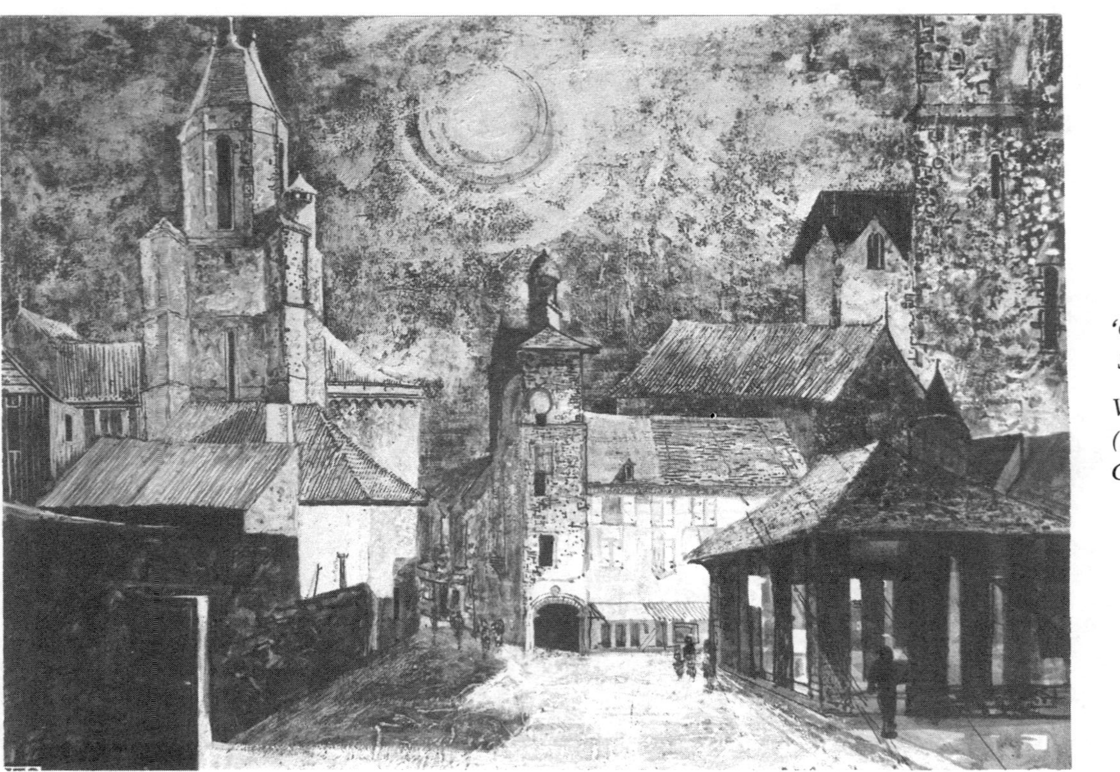

'Cadomin Market'
S.W. France.

Watercolour. 1973, (R.A.). Private Collection.

time to think, as well as a time to sleep and dream.

Travelling on a canal is a lovely experience; but it needs two active men to work the locks. This can be difficult if the lock-keeper, now a dwindling race, is no longer living in the nearby cottage which means you do the work yourself. Letting the water out is a simple operation as it lowers quite smoothly a fully laden péniche or cruiser. Filling up the lock needs care in controlling the rush of water from a higher level. It can also mean climbing an iron ladder to mount the high wall and so up to ground level to operate the sluice on each gate. This means that the pilot must be cautious in controlling the boat against the fierce onrush of water as the sluice from each gate is raised. This often needs a boatman with a pole to keep the vessel from crashing into the stone sides of the lock. We were with a little party of six when one member fell into the swirling water while our engine was running which we quickly switched off to prevent our friend from injury by the propeller. There were times when the lock master, living in his cottage, was sufficiently enterprising to have attractive home grown vegetable, fruit and other provisions for sale which others, like us, much appreciated.

Since the commercial use of the canals as a means of transport has declined, nature has asserted its autonomy. As a result, the adjacent countryside is lush and verdant, the wild flowers abundant to delight any botanist. Once you leave the assembly quay at Castelnoudray and move towards the first lock, a sensation of release form the confusion and complexities of the twentieth century comes as 'manner in the wilderness'. You drop with pleasure into a low gear accentuated by the slow smooth movement of the cabin cruiser. This reaction is not necessarily shared by all the cruising community, judging by the loud music coming from some!

The towing path, which once formed a soft surface for so many working horses to trudge along, is now an ideal cycle track upon which teenagers can race along from one lock to another. But this sport did not interfere with the tranquillity of our days. It was seeing distant Carcasonne in a translucent atmosphere that gave the ancient city a transformation into an unreal existence more closely related to the paintings of the Limburg Brothers than the twentieth century. A reminder, as if we needed one, of the change in the working lives of so many who once lived by the transport industry related to the canal! This reminder was a chapel close to the canal bank built to serve the needs of the watermen who stopped to rest their horses and refresh themselves after a particularly long, hot day. The chapel must have been a half-way pause but I did wonder who officiated in a remote chapel, or who was responsible for the building. This little structure is featured in one of my large watercolours.

Our second cruise was for six: Doreen, Gordon, Margaret, Philip, Eileen and myself which meant a much larger cruiser. Doreen was first aboard, choosing the best cabin and loudly announced the fact. The rest of us shook ourselves into the remaining bunks and prepared for a good rest after the days labours in the heat. It was a good holiday after which Margaret and Philip went home. The du Midi had a branch canal which must not be forgotten because it passes through Montaubon. The town's most famous citizen was Ingres where a large collection of his drawings are in the Musée Ingres. One of the reasons for our interest was the fact that the museum had a splendid work by Goya. We returned the next year to see this painting again but it had gone – we imagined, to increase the collection of a more important city, so you 'rob Peter in order to pay a replete Paul'!, or that is how it seems.

We three had a few days on which to loiter; but where should we go? We were not too far from Caranac. It seemed a good idea, Meem phoned Madame to see if she could accommodate us. She could, so off we went. We were looking forward to an interesting termination to our few weeks in France and this was ideal. This medieval village-cum-town of Caranac, is a wonderful survival, architecturally, of a number of timber framed buildings unrivalled for variety and size. Fortunately, the main road passes above the village and this has kept the community free from the developers. The only developers are settlers who have bought and restored buildings in an appreciative way and possibly saved them from decay. There are still a few by the river which are in need of conservation. The Romanesque Abbey Church and nearby structures are exceptionally fine. The sculpture and tympanum over the west door are splendid examples of the work of the twelfth century – the Mise en Tompe being a very rare survival, particularly as it has not, in any way, been vandalised.

Caranac has been the subject for many of my drawings and paintings. In so many ways this is a dream village. When sitting, drawing by the riverside, one breathes in the stillness, the smell of the river under a slight mist, the whole atmosphere whispering of its long history, of people in love and in sadness. I hope there are a few pictures of mine that communicate the meaning and purpose of the paintings to those who can read my language. My pictures of Caranac were just a few works inspired by our annual visits to rural France over a period of twenty-five years. In every case, they were very productive, enjoyed and shared by life long friends. John and Polly Eden (John a war-time friend I had lost touch with suddenly) appeared on our drive to Bordeaux in a car just in front of us. This inaugurated a few trips in their company which produced a number of very amusing incidents. One overnight stop in an auberge contained very doubtful plumbing. The showers were situated across the landing right opposite our bedrooms. In the early hours John roused us with the expression, 'Get up dears, we have of the water from India, some ***** fellow did not turn off the shower'.

On another occasion, we spent a lovely day or two in Pierre les Fontaines. The hotel, formally a medieval castle had been used as a prison during the German occupation. All the doors were covered with steel plates making them very heavy to open or close. The patron was a very forceful character. In the courtyard, with a fountain in the centre, he had prepared a sumptuous supper with plenty of wine plus a post-prandial ouzo. Meem could not manage all that was poured out for her so surreptitiously emptied her glass onto the paving. She was sitting next to a French woman with her little girl, the liquid on the paving was seen by the mother who thought her daughter was responsible which prompted the exclamation, 'Oh, la, la!' The same evening, Dorelia was encouraged to play a piece by Chopin on an antique piano, followed by Polly, cap sideways on, singing a cockney song with suitable actions. This received tremendous applause. Later on that evening, our patron asked Polly if she slept with her husband, saying if not, he would be pleased to oblige! These were the days before the proliferation of luxury hotels when the country auberge was the place to meet, enjoy and share an essential element of French country life.

IX
DORELIA AND IAN

AT THE TURN OF THE LAST CENTURY, about 1910, the art schools and colleges taught drawing by means of a dim and mistaken theory that the slavish copying of classical plaster casts of Greek and Roman statues and architectural details, was the best way to acquire skill, especially when shading (as it was called) with the aid of a tightly rolled paper smugger. Quite a number of students going to the Slade School – Henry Tonks, Augustus John, Stanley Spencer – were, with others, associated with a movement to change this effete system, designed to kill and not stimulate.

It was John, with his fluent, sensitive, powerful draughtsmanship, with others, who lead the way into a new century. Roger Fry organised the first Post-Impressionist exhibition to be seen in London which created a storm of unjust abuse. John's character was a mixture of energy and fluctuating interests causing a number of large paintings, important commissions and projects left unfinished, but the drawings and etching are complete in themselves as statements of rhythm and form, stamped with the mark of authority; many of which are of his wife Dorelia. One of the most penetrating and sensitive portraits of Dorelia as an old lady in oil on canvas has all the qualities of a great painting. But our Dorelia, so named because of our admiration for John's drawings and because we loved the

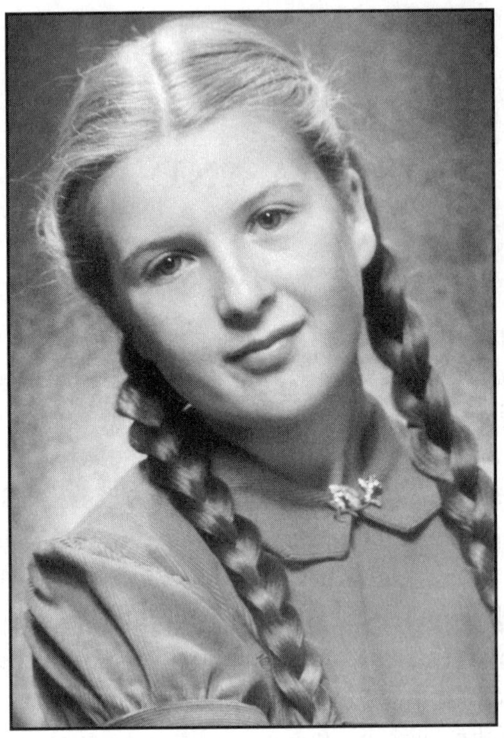

Our daughter Dorelia

name, was born in Oxford during my absence in France. Because of this I did not see very much of her babyhood. It was a wonderful time when Eileen was able to spend short periods with me in Ripon. She has some extraordinary comments on feeding babies from the two elderly spinsters with whom she was staying. They were fatuous and fanciful but so well meaning. These early years were unfortunately left to Eileen's cares and up-bringing of Dorelia, so it is easy to imagine my feelings on being home for good after what seemed to be a lifetime. Eileen and I were both teaching at the Technical High School for Girls until I moved to London, but a Mrs. Kilbey took care of Dorelia after school until we got home. The system worked well with no complaints from Dorelia. Of course, she had her pets; Binky the black rabbit was the first, although I am sorry to say it did not live very long, but the hamster that lived in the airing cupboard stayed the course after being resuscitated by Eileen with a sniff of brandy!

Russell House, Dorelia's prep school, was just out of the village, opposite the railway station. There were other children of her age – Jennifer Ling, the Whyte's boy, John from Picmoss and pupils from further afield – so Dorelia had friends and was happy there I think. It was interesting to note Dorelia's growth by the amount that her head showed above the parapet of the bridge as she approached the front gate. These were the days of David Crocket, America's Robin Hood. Corinne, Eileen's goddaughter, was having a short stay with us and she was a David Crocket fan. Dorelia and she hit it off, helped by a tent erected under the apple tree. Corinne boasted a David Crocket hat with a rabbit tail hanging down the back. It was fun while it lasted but died when Corinne left. My pencil and wash drawing of Bridge Cottage shows the tent under the apple tree with Rufus, our Red Setter, asleep. By 1953 it was time to move on. Dorelia had outgrown Russell House and was ready for the next stage. I cannot remember what the circumstances were that led us to Micklefield a boarding school in Sussex. The problem of fees was very much a problem, but Eileen's father was a great help and took an interest in Dorelia's progress.

I had one major problem, the car. Now cars were like gold dust. Few, very few were on the market as industry was in the process of changing from the production of armaments to the needs of a rapidly altered world. But I did manage to locate a garage in North London that had a grey Austin truck for sale so I went up, bought it, and drove, for the first time, a truck through the London suburbs and so home. We had some good times in our truck. I had a cover made and seats put down the sides, but when we drove down to Seaford we parked our commercial transport in a side road. On one of our holidays we spent some time in Cirenchester and the Cotswolds. This meant having passengers in the rear seats so we invented a simple means of communication. At each end of a thin piece of rubber tubing we pushed the end of a plastic funnel. When passed through a gap in the passenger seat's window it worked admirably.

We liked Micklefield – its education policy and the way girls grew into young women with a certain confidence and poise. But the times were weighed heavily against these small independent schools. Micklefield was later forced into amalgamation with a similar establishment outside Seaford but was only one of many which have gone, leaving nothing to mark their previous existences. This surely is a sign of the times where independence is giving way to dependence on every conceivable organisation from the government downwards. Like 'the child in the pram', we are demanding 'rights' before having earned them.

After eight happy years in Micklefield Dorelia decided to investigate a possible career in art. So, in September 1961, she joined the first years at Maidstone College of Art. Her lithographs, of which we have examples, were very good, showing clearly her grasp of overprinting and the method of procedure for obtaining the impact of a powerful print. Her natural feeling for good craftsmanship was particularly apparent in ceramic work and hand-built pottery. She instinctively knew what a suitable form of decoration was for specific shapes, volumes and size, or none at all. We thought they were fine objects to be preserved at all costs, being unique works produced during her time at Goldsmiths from 1963–5. It seems to me that these large clay pots were made for themselves without a thought being given to commercial reproductive needs, fashions or borrowed themes. I am so glad that Russell and Jolyon (known to us as Jo) have examples of Dorelia's large works. By 1965 Dorelia had started an Art Teacher's Certificate (ATC); completing this in 1966 she spent a year teaching at Swadeland's School in Lenham. This must have been uneventful for little is recorded of her time there.

At a friend's party Dorelia met Eric Nearn and married him in 1965. After the ceremony at All Saints, Hollingbourne, the breakfast was at Brushings. We had gone to the expense of hiring a marquee in case of rain but the day proved to be fine which caused Dorelia to complain that the expensive marquee was not being used! At this time Eric was a manager of a public house in the City but they wanted a business of their own and when they saw The Ringlestone was on the market, they made a bid and acquired this wayside inn at great expense. The Ringlestone had been owned by an ageing mother and daughter, both alcoholics. Their language and behaviour were quite intolerably abusive. The building was in need of urgent overhaul and repair, but it had considerable potential. So Dorelia, with Eric, began the work that lasted about sixteen years. The two vital jobs were the roof and the kitchen wall which had an ominous crack. Eric agreed with me that a substantial buttress was needed so this was the first task we worked on and as far as I know it was the answer. No wall has collapsed after twenty years! Job two was the roof; but not for us! It was necessary to pay a roofing contractor to do the work for which our assistance came in handy. The floors above the bars were very unstable and needed vertical support with which we were able to help.

A magnificent barn with great double doors for the entrance of a haywain was adjacent to our garden and we suffered as the farmer was persuaded by an employed pig-minder to demolish the barn as the pigs had severely damaged the ground level structure. I witnessed this vandalism with horror especially when I saw these great beams being towed away and burnt. I was so angry I asked Bob, the foreman, if I could have some. This enabled me to store about seven beams in the garage. They have all been used to good purpose since.

Improvements to The Ringlestone continued, as did the clientele, as the house became more hospitable. Russell was born in 1968, followed by Jo in 1970. They have both grown into two super men. I nearly said young men but they are now passing the 'young' stage I fear. They are as different as chalk from cheese. Russell was academic and did well at King's School, Rochester and after a short pause took a Master's Degree at Reading University. We think he would make a splendid husband but early disappointments can cut deep, sometimes permanently, we still hope not in his case. Jo was not in any way interested in books but in Lego and similar constructive toys he was a wizard, solving such problems by instinct and rapidly. He now has three lovely boys and an equally lovely wife. Jo worked for the builders' merchants Perkins for some time but became very dissatisfied and with his father-in-law's support started his own business in 'tool hire' which I believe is going well as we all thought it would.

In 1983 Eric and Jo went for a cycle ride down the lane near home when a tragedy happened. Eric suffered a severe heart attack from which he died instantly, leaving little Jo to hurry back and tell Dorelia. It was my unpleasant duty to identify the body later. The result for Dorelia was devastating; a business to run with two boys to educate. The boys, being brought up in a rural area had several friends with whom they spent much time. There was Anna, more man than woman, who lived in an isolated cottage in a meadow across the lane from The Ringlestone. She worked with a Mr Davison who bred bullocks and dealt in logs which were delivered to us to burn in the open hearth in our inglenook. I think these neighbours must have been helpful to Dorelia. In an oblique way she coped (we do not know how) with a situation to test anyone's character. Time has shown our daughter had plenty. She ran The Ringlestone single handed, with what help we could give, for almost a year before the business was sold in 1983. Dorelia then moved into a cottage on Platt's Heath where certain repairs and the cleaning up other people's mess, required an oak support which was where another one of my salvaged beams found a resting place. This was a hard time for Dorelia. She did all kinds of menial jobs just to keep going. To add insult to injury the cottage was burgled and a set of valuable plates stolen while Dorelia was at work packing apples!

But better things were on their way. She had met Ian a number of times as he frequented the pub with one or two friends. The signals of mutual attraction must have passed between them when Ian was on leave from his Cunard ship because in 1987 they married. Brushings was made to look lovely, but no marquee this time! In 1986 they inspected Forge House, which is in Ruckinge, almost Romney Marsh, and bought it. It is another late medieval house with a most chequered history. Lots of restoration here but of the enjoyable kind when you see an obvious way to rectify the stupidity of previous inhabitants. One of the most important was the removal of an ugly modern fireplace of around the 1960s which was filling the space of an open fire made obvious by the bresermer visible to anyone knowing what it was and its

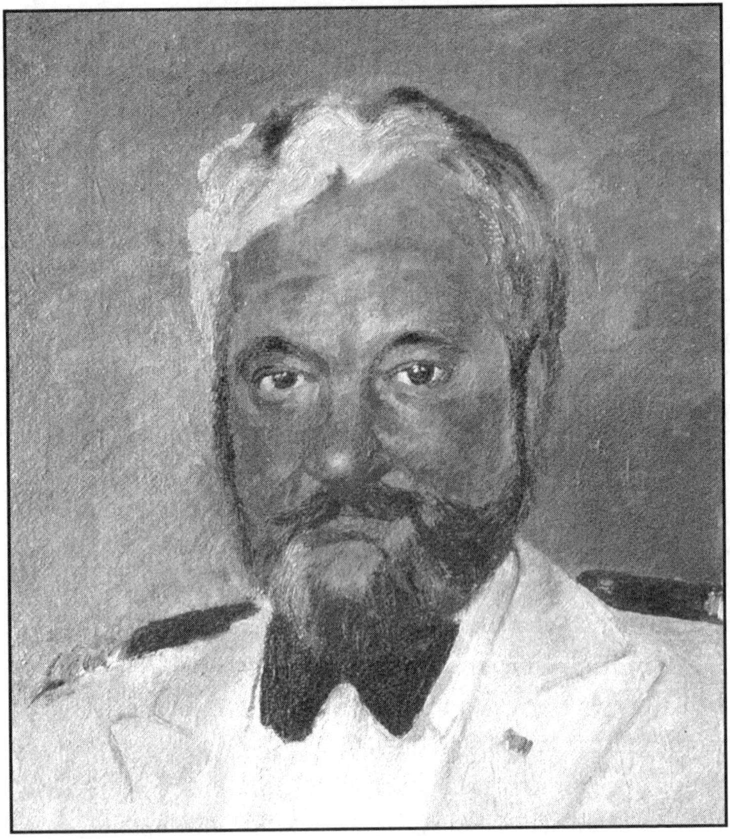

Ian Burrell, Dorelia's second husband

function. So Dorelia had the hideous fireplace removed and lo there was the inglenook, in a sorry state. Once repaired with good brickwork by a sympathetic craftsman, a hood installed, a fire basket on the hearth, and made a feature that fitted the house perfectly. A main ceiling beam had its end built into the old fire place because it needed vertical support! This is where my last timber was used, one in each of the three houses in which Dorelia had lived.

From 1986–1988 we enjoyed wonderful French holidays which deserve a chapter of their own. During these years, with the building of the new railway and international station at Ashford, the town changed in character and appearance. Building and rebuilding houses by the thousand have brought an unlovely present in what was once a charming market town of the past. After considerable thought, Dorelia and Ian decided to move. It was a surprise to us, but absolutely understandable. As one ambulance driver said to me the government is 'putting cart before horse', houses but no roads, no schools, no surgery, no garage, no sewage, electricity. I imagine these essentials will come later! But Ashford is fast becoming a great place to get away from and Dorelia and Ian have done the right thing in giving up medievalism for a new house in Maidstone which they see as a temporary arrangement for the time being. Needless to say, Dorelia and Ian have been a tremendous help in our move from Broad Street. It was a painful wrench about which I shall have more to record in due course.

So the one last thing to be recorded here is Dorelia and Ian's move to Maidstone into 36 Marigold Way. As Ian said sardonically, 'What a name', but the house is fine and suits their purpose admirably. No one can pretend that Dorelia has had an easy, free from problems life. Meem and I did a lot of travelling on the *Orpheus* and in association with it, ten visits to Arizona. We had nothing to hinder our coming and going. It has not been the same, exactly, for Dorelia. She and Ian now have the opportunity to have an extended holiday in

Australia and New Zealand. We are pleased they are going especially as they have taken the trouble to make a map of the journey for us to study and to know where they are. There will no doubt be much to add when they are home again.

X

WE MOVE TO KENT

FOR A LONG TIME I HAD BEEN SICK OF LONDON but saw little hope of a change. Meem had moved out of Springfield into Sittingbourne leaving a gap in the Inspectorate team. Then I saw the advertisement for an Art Inspector in Kent. I applied, not expecting success. I wanted that job and I got it with intense pleasure and relief.

I could see there was much to do. The few reproductions round the balcony, where carols were sung before the Christmas break, were faded and dirty. When I changed these for a pair of my large oil paintings there were low murmurings of disapproval, to my amazement – no one wanted change!

Then I had a shock. There was an elderly lady with white hair, spending her time at great expense wrapping up little pictures in tissue paper of Peter Pan and other banalities. It was time I put into practice all that I knew from my experience in London and I tried to order, through County Supplies, a sample of stacking frames. But they had no idea what was needed either in design or cost. So, I went up to Sheridon Knoles in Hackney, who supplied London County Council, and arranged for them to send a similar product to Kent which they were very pleased to do. These frames were designed to fit in tens in a box made for the purpose. Now, the Peter Pan reproductions have been disposed of and forgotten.

My visits took me to distant parts of the county and I realised how very seldom, if ever, the children were taken to an art gallery. The second best was to take the pictures to them – an altruistic idea – but I learned that, 'You can take a horse to water but you cannot make him drink'. In too many cases I had misunderstood the situation in some schools For example, the end wall of a secondary school hall was decorated with five little china ducks! In this instance I was able to commission a large, six foot by two foot six inches, woven decoration which I had the pleasure of seeing take the place of the ducks. But was it ever cleaned? The revised scheme was to supply a secondary school with two boxes, each box to contain five reproductions of one work; one in colour and the other four details in black and white. These were commissioned photographs, approximately fourteen inches by nine inches, of excellent quality, showing details of the work. Each box provided material for a talk on the artists displayed. One school I visited had hung the pictures in a busy corridor where they were most unlikely to be seen, never mind examined, except by an indolent who tried to peel the picture from the frame but was not left long enough to complete the job! This observation made me realise that examination of boxes on their return would be a future necessity. One headmaster took delivery of a box of pictures and chose one for his room. The secretary had her pick and the rest were divided one for each classroom. This was how carefully chosen material was made useless since the picture had been fragmented into meaningless parts. It was to combat this type of ignorance that the guide was written. I wonder how many other schools failed to understand the purpose of this service or miss it now it has gone.

Organising such a comprehensive service was a full time activity. Going to London to select items for the boxes meant visiting the National Gallery, Victoria and Albert Museum and other galleries for more contemporary work. As the number of boxes grew it became essential to compile a catalogue which grew into the idea of a book production. This is where John Haynes authorised an assistant for me and we worked together on the first volume. The majority of the artists catalogued had a self portrait to head the notes. This was a considerable task for an overworked photographer on the premises, but the first volume, with John's foreword, was published in 1971. Volume two followed soon afterwards. The next request from John was would I organise a Kent schools' art and craft exhibition and could it be done ready for the autumn? The answer was, 'No, give me a year, all of which I shall need to do the job to our satisfaction'. I had to make a complete survey of the county, locating where art and crafts of a good standard could be found. I began in Thanet, then Sheppey, then worked my way back to Maidstone. It threw up interesting results and I began to visualise the kind of exhibition we could present to the county. Joan Chartton of Sittingbourne College was most helpful, being full of energy and enthusiasm. I began to select items which might be useful for display. I had seen the former ballroom in the New Metropole, Folkestone, which had been set aside for the exhibition. The timetable made sure the work would be ready for collection in time, in plenty of time for display. Pottery, textiles and paintings were going to look fine once the display and arrangements were tackled. So I was pleased when John came into the office to announce that Lord Kenneth Clarke had agreed to open the exhibition and had invited us both to lunch.

So John and I turned up at the Gatehouse, the only part now used, in what must have been a very busy castle, with knights planning the murder of Thomas Beckett! We were shown quite a number of Lord Kenneth's treasures including a fine oil painting by Turner over the fireplace, which he said he had bought for a few hundred pounds when Turner was unpopular. It was the same work, now worth several millions that had caused such a rumpus amongst his relatives when Lord Kenneth died. It was a free and easy day – I cannot remember where the food came from (I do not think it was Chinese takeaway!), but I do remember the wine decanter being slid down the polished table top (rather as a whisky bottle is slid along the bar top in westerns) with the comment, 'It's only plonk'! The only table decoration was a small Henry Moore sculpture. After we were taken for a walk round the battlements (just my cup of tea!) we were led to the cloakroom where priceless prints by Dürer hung. Naturally I felt pleased that the exhibition would be worthy of his time. Ah, but was it? A few days before the exhibition was due to be opened John came into the office, all smiles. Lord Kenneth regrets, etc, etc, but was going to Spain to open the Guggenheim Centre. 'Oh', I said, 'what a pity. So will you take his place and open the exhibition?' 'No,' John said, 'you will'. So that is what I had to do, and did.

Because of the demise of the Kent Education Committee together with all the Inspectors, this exhibition, for which we had hoped so much, had, like the circulating scheme, disintegrated into obscurity. It was the first and the last. All the time, energy, expertise, and money spent on two major projects was thrown away and, in the case of the circulating scheme, given away. But this means nothing to blinkered, bigoted, ignorant politicians as will be demonstrated later on. As far as I am aware, the National Curriculum does not mention the arts which are so basic for the development of the sensibilities. I understand 'culture' to mean a trained and refined state of awareness of manners and history, awareness of the wide spectrum of human knowledge and the ability to benefit there-by. If this is a reasonable summary, why does the BBC advertise a programme called Knife Culture? I thought the illegal use of knives in society was a 'crime' and not a 'culture'! The misuse of words for euphemistic purposes, especially in advertising, is becoming more common of which Knife Culture is a good example.

A pleasant piece of correspondence came one morning in the form of an invitation for me to join the college staff in the annual celebration of Saint Catherine's Day in Oxford, she being the patron saint of the college. The date for this event coincided with the time we were to spend on the Orpheus. So I had to decline, thinking that this was the last I should hear, but no! The following year the invitation was repeated. So I arranged with Meem to book us into a hotel in Abingdon. The hotel was built into and over a watermill that once formed part of Abingdon Abbey. The accommodation was pleasant and comfortable but the weather was not. I got myself dressed in plenty of time, in black tie of course, and waited in the lounge for my taxi. The taxi did not come. I waited and waited and watched the time going by, but still no taxi. So the telephone was used in an effort to obtain some information and some bright spark said the taxi was on its way, but with no indication of which way! At last transport came and we set off in mist and drizzle. Outside Oxford we were caught in a horrid traffic jam at a huge roundabout where progress was slow, as the driver seemed to notice! But minutes were ticking away before we continued in a leisurely manner towards Oxford. On entering the city the taxi driver became quite confused. He had no idea where St. Catherines was located so I knew I was going to be late. Then, quite suddenly, at the end of a long brick wall and a few more twists and turns I was there, or almost. I found my way across a soaking wet lawn towards a brightly lit room that was swarming with black ties, so I knew I was in the right place. Pre-prandials were being administered to the black ties while Dr. Orme took me to a small exhibition of very mediocre watercolours done by the master of the college? A portrait of one of the returning masters by the artist sat opposite to me at the top table next to the master. I have often thought, looking back to that evening, that I was not sufficiently appreciative or generous enough as I should have been. Did the master wish to be made an Honorary Member of the RWS (Royal Watercolour Society)? I could have inquired from Dr. Orme, but I did not.

At a given signal we all rose, picked up our napkins and wandered off for dessert and coffee. I sat next to a 'fellow' who was very affable and talked about the book he was writing. Then it was time for carriages, cabs or taxis. Dr. Orme took my arm as we walked over the same soaking wet lawn to my taxi and so back to the hotel where Meem was waiting. The time of my return I have now forgotten, except that it was late.

It was at this time that each county, with government backing, wanted a University, or were persuaded into the need. Whatever the reason, a University was founded at Canterbury. As recorded, we entertained Mrs. Templeman, wife of the new chancellor on their arrival in Kent. I met the chancellor once or twice at meetings in the University. A few years later it opened some sort of vague arts committee with what I thought were unspecified aims. One member of the select few(!) was the prophet of 'concrete poetry' which I never had explained so I have never understood what connection there was between this kind of verse, and sand and cement! These visual arts committee meetings acquainted me with the new University buildings. The little I saw struck me as being rather mediocre, the staircases narrow, with the 'going' too short and the 'risers' rather steep. Our committee room was small and cramped; giving the impression that too much had been done with inadequate means. Perhaps if I should go back now I might have different views.

Two of my visits are memorable. On leaving the main building we passed a hall and my companion, a committee member, said, 'That jazz band has been practising that all day and they've still got it wrong'. The second report on student activity I thought was a poor reflection on their behaviour. A loan exhibition of work of some value was disapproved of by the student body so they took the exhibition down and hid the items in cupboards and behind lavatory seats. I am not cognizant of the final outcome but I remember thinking, 'What price education?'. On the other hand, students' pranks at The Royal College were often quite funny and harmless. There was the occasion when a small bag of flour was let down on the head of a speaker at a monthly critique. Such energies had their culmination in the Chelsea Arts Ball which in the 1930s and '40s was one of the great carnival spectacles mounted by students of different colleges during their final year.

Responsibility for the Kent Inspectorate was, like most other county authorities, concerned with the running of short courses for in-service teachers, a subject I mentioned when speaking of Meem's long drive to Kingsgate. All such courses were now centred in Eversley College in Folkestone, causing extra traffic up and down the A20. The college had a resident warden who, with his wife, kept the building in good order, supervised the kitchen and prepared rooms. The presentation of all meals was very civilised, the lounge area large and comfortable, as was the dining room, the bedrooms were also very pleasant.

Most of the larger courses were carefully planned and interesting, to which some well-known personalities were invited to address the assembled company. On one of my courses the speaker was Sir Charles Wheeler PRA. At the end of the session I remember John Haynes walking Sir Charles over to where two of my pictures were hanging. I have no idea what passed between them but from a scrap of conversation I overheard I think John thought I would be an ARA by Christmas! What is not known is the need to be approved by the members of the RA and ARA club in order to secure their votes when elections take place. This is the way in, but I have never been a member nor am I ever likely to be. In a few instances, artists who have made a national or international reputation receive an invitation to full membership of the Academy but have declined. Can you imagine Picasso being pleased to become an RA?

Another event which had lasting repercussions was an exhibition I held at the New Metropole, Folkestone – a newly acquired property of Sir Gerald Glovers. For some unknown reason Sir Gerald and I got on well (he took a shine to me, as Ian might say). He said, 'I know, I'll throw a party and you invite ten friends and I will do the same'. The evening was arranged and an enjoyable time was had at his expense. At the end, before leaving he said to me, 'Ernest, if you ever find yourself in a fix just give me call'. It was a statement I never forgot.

XI

THE ROYAL SOCIETY OF PAINTERS IN WATERCOLOURS

IN THE LATE SIXTIES OR EARLY SEVENTIES, Dick Cowern RA asked me if I would apply for membership to the RWS. This was something I had never thought of, not knowing anything about the society or precisely for what it stood. Anyway, I submitted work and to my surprise was elected. I learned afterwards that to be elected first time was unusual! The Society had its home in Conduit Street. My first reaction to the Society and its activities was that it was not what I thought it should be for a Royal Society. Malcolm and Ruth Fry laboured for the Society with unparalleled loyalty. Robert Austin RA was an ageing President who was seldom seen and I am afraid did less in spite of the fact that, as I could see, the Society was running into dire trouble.

The golden days of watercolour painting were long past as I was to learn in due course. The artist's suppers were anything but sumptuous – the member's donated food was served on paper plates and wine was drunk from cups or plastic mugs that would safely hold liquids. Meem and I were shocked by the situation especially when we saw Ruth having to cope single-handedly with a coffee urn. So Meem and I decided to do something. We presented the Society with its first Burgundy wine glasses, enough for the few members who attended the suppers. Austin had to be nudged by Malcolm to acknowledge the gift. We then had a go at table laying and decorations for the luncheon. We supplied paper serviettes and Eileen arranged bowls of flowers down the table centre. Nothing was said, not in my hearing, but we hope some notice had been taken.

Things were getting quite serious for the RWS – too many members were 'getting on' and could not be relied upon to do much, if anything. Andrew Freeth RA was elected President when Austin had a stroke and retired but he and Malcolm fell out as Andrew took over Malcolm's chair and office. So Andrew was elbowed out. Then what happened? Another election. Wilfred Fairclough and a few others asked me if I would stand. Not expecting anything from the question as there were many senior members more eligible, I agreed and to my surprise was promptly elected in 1976. Then, and only then, did Malcolm explain the grim reality; the total assets did not exceed three thousand pounds and there were only three years of our lease left. What had I let myself in for? Something unexpected; but conditions generally made the information hardly surprising. Malcolm had a friend or two in top administration and we formed a working party with the prime object of raising money.

Our first move was to let the gallery to Sotheby's between our own exhibitions. This produced a welcome addition to the kitty. Our second move was a disaster. Our chief advisors introduced us to a professional fund raising company and assured us that their guidance ought to help solve the money problem. So representatives of the firm moved into Malcolm's office, took over his chair and phone and began to turn out folders providing statistics of the errors of asking for too little. Small sums must be avoided as it inhibits generosity. We were favoured with blue coloured booklets but nothing positive as a strategy for raising money. We got sick of this and dismissed those employed using our premises. The final result was a bill for ten thousand pounds for services rendered which just about gobbled up our earnings from Sotheby's!

So we started again on our own. We designed all advertising matter, appeal notices, information leaflets and Malcolm enjoyed supervising and correcting our own materials. We did well I think to raise one hundred and seventy five thousand pounds – enough to secure another home for the RWS. But where and how? Various ideas were suggested in the search for new premises including a direct appeal to the Queen. Although this was thought inappropriate, an approach was made to the Secretary of State for the Environment regarding accommodation at Kensington Palace but the Society was informed that space there was fully allocated. An approach to the Society for the Protection of Ancient Buildings was equally fruitless. Then I had a thought: Gerald Glover. So I rang Sir Gerald, reminding him of our previous meeting in the New Metropole and that I was now PRWS. looking for a gallery to replace Conduit Street. He invited me to his house, just off Park Lane. The evening was awful on that day – it rained and rained through a cold mist and a chilly breeze as everything was wrapped in gloom. I found his small house and was let in, wet and cold, by an elderly housekeeper and taken to a warm sitting room with a blazing fire. It was cosy and hospitable. I had not been sitting long when there was a pitter-patter of slippers on the stairs as Sir Gerald came down. His welcome was friendly, almost avuncular as he sat down to ask how he could help. I could only briefly outline the problem of finding new premises for the

RWS the import of which he grasped at once. He said that his company had secured the development contract for the South Bank and the Southwark Council had expressed the view that an educational element would be most welcome. Sir Gerald smiled, lifted the phone and spoke to his architect. I heard him say, 'I have the President of the Royal Watercolour Society here. Could we help by including a gallery in our planning? The Society is looking for new premises.' Our need fitted snugly into the overall scheme so it looked as if our gallery problem was going to be solved. These were the first steps towards the establishment of a gallery on the site even though the space itself had originally been designated as a supermarket.

With only £3,000 in the bank and the Society's main asset – its Conduit Street lease – decreasing in value by the day the RWS soon had little choice. The only alternative, which was advocated by some members who saw a danger in moving from the West End, was to join the Federation of British Artists. But such a move would have been disastrous: the identity of the Society would have been lost. On 26 February 1975 the Select Committee of the Society unanimously passed a resolution recommending that the RWS accept without delay Southwark Council's offer of a sixty-year lease in the new building of a new home together with offices and stores for a nominal sum of £60,000. The Royal Society of Painter-Etchers and Engravers also decided that they now wished to be equal partners in any new venture with the RWS rather than tenants and eventually the lease for the new Bankside Gallery was signed. However, other problems that needed a solution were just round the corner.

In order to ensure that the funds were legally used a trust had to be set up and someone found to help bring together and chair a body of trustees. By chance I came upon a copy of a lecture given to the Chelsea Arts Club by Nicholas Stacey. On reading the script, *Living in an Alibi Society* (a treatise in which he roundly condemned the modern practice of blaming others and avoiding responsibility for one's own actions), it occurred to me that Stacey might be interesting in becoming involved with the RWS. I wrote to Stacey who in his reply suggested that I contact his chairman, Francis Singer. So I wrote to Francis and in due course things progressed to the point where we thought the RWS and Royal Society of Painter-Printmakers (RES) should meet. This was duly arranged by a luncheon party on 29 January 1979 to be held at the Painters' Hall in the city. This luncheon was hosted by Rodney Millard (President of the Institute of Practitioners in Advertising) and the menu was as follows:

Smoked Trout
Chateau De Viré 1974
Gooseberry relish

Fillet of Beef Wellington
Mouton Cadet 1976
Béarnaise sauce
Buttered courgettes
Braised celery
French beans
Sauté potatoes

Selection of English cheeses
Pippins

Fresh Fruit

Coffee Taylors Port
Hine VSOP

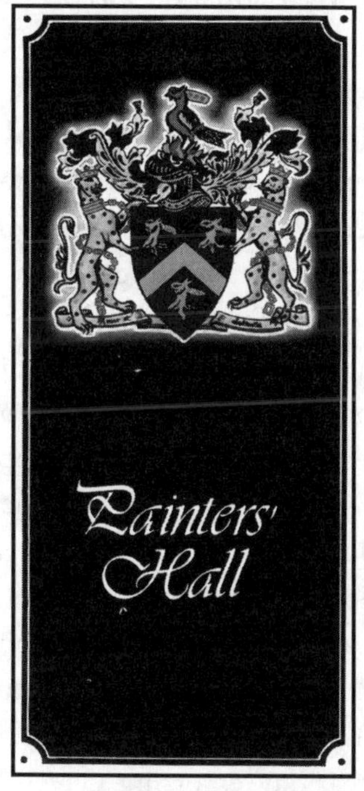

The outcome was satisfactory and Francis became our first Chairman of Trustees, a position he held for several years, holding a number of meetings in the splendid boardroom of his company Central and Sheerwood in Belgravia. He managed to collect a number of political and industrial figures (Lord Seebohm, Stacey, Harry Eccleston, Norman St John Stevas, Lord Sir John Stephus, Nicholas Stacey, Lord Forté) who discussed ways and means of achieving a total of one million pounds for the Royal Watercolour Society's new gallery at Bankside. It did not materialise but it did bring the Society out of the obscurity of Conduit Street into the awareness and interest of many prominent people. Francis himself made a goodwill gesture of a gift to the Society of £6,000 worth of shares in his own company. The Society was moving forwards slowly as inflation was producing escalating costs and we were forced to reduce the size of the gallery by omitting the basement for storage and some administration which was a sad loss. During this upheaval Malcolm went to the bank to deposit some cash when the manager said, 'Mr Fry, we have been going through the vaults and have come across this, is it yours?', handing him a rather dirty parcel wrapped in string. Malcolm did not recognise the parcel but the two of them untied the string and found a triangular red box which contained the RWS chain of office which had been lost for nearly forty years. This happened to be in the important year of my presidency. I was the President who wore the gift of Queen Victoria, designed and made by the Bavarian Sir Herbert Herkomer in 1849, for the first time after all those years of obscurity. I mentioned this chain of office when welcoming Her Majesty, Queen Elizabeth II on the morning of 11 November 1980, when she opened the gallery. This was a great day, escorting Queen Elizabeth round a special exhibi-

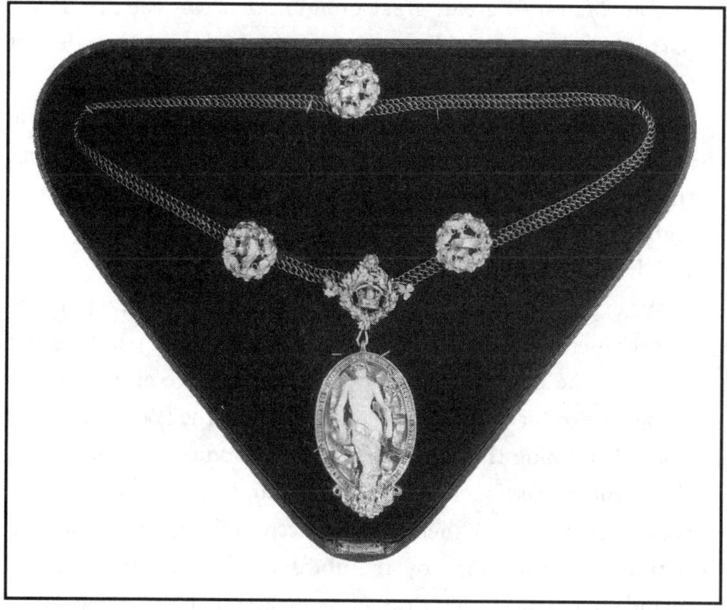

The RWS chain of office

tion of watercolours by Turner. Her Majesty was intrigued by a work in which Turner had painted Windsor Castle in the welsh mountains, giving this splendid building a new mystery. This is what I said in my speech:

> Your Majesty
> As President of the Royal Society of Painters in Watercolours and, on this occasion, speaking also for the Royal Society of Painter-Etchers and Engravers, it is my honour to welcome you most warmly to this new gallery on Bankside. [. . .]
>
> The creation of this new gallery has only been made possible by the devoted and cooperative effort of a few dedicated people. They have looked past the innumerable problems, with their attendant doubts and uncertainties, to a permanent re-establishment here of an essentially British institution.

Your Majesty's great, great grandmother was the first Royal patron of the Royal Watercolour Society. I am reminded of Queen Victoria each time I wear this gold and ivory chain of office, for she presented it to the society in 1892. It is in the style of Art-Nouveau and serves to remind us of the Society's past and the successive phases of aesthetic fashions in the last eighty-eight years which are representative of some of the traditions which are a part of the Society's history.

We expect the Bankside Gallery to become the focal point to an ever increasing public interested in watercolour painting and prints of the past, present and future. Plans are already being made for exhibitions which will demonstrate the Societies' intentions of stepping through the barriers of traditional concepts to those encompassing new approaches and techniques. We are concerned to widen their field of activity beyond the normal pattern of exhibitions by members of the two Societies, to include open and group displays from artists in other countries. We are looking for ways of disseminating new ideas and the imaginative use of modern materials; not only to stimulate our own members, but to create additional public interest in order to widen the frontiers of aesthetic enjoyment and thus contribute to a greater human understanding.

As patron of the Royal Society of Painters in Watercolour we hope that you, Ma'am, will share our pride in this achievement and feel a response towards those aims of this gallery which I have so very briefly outlined. It has a most distinguished body of trustees, a director without whom none of this would have been possible and enthusiastic members of two societies who are dedicated to its future.

There would be no way more appropriate to mark this important day for our two Societies than our receiving Your Majesty here this afternoon to open the Bankside Gallery and the inaugural exhibition of works by JMW Turner. May I request Ma'am that you now honour us with this unveiling?

BUCKINGHAM PALACE

11th November, 1980

Dear Mr Greenwood,

When we returned to Buckingham Palace The Queen told me to write to thank you for arranging the opening ceremony at the new Gallery this afternoon and to congratulate you on organising a most successful and agreeable engagement. The Queen, as your Patron, was delighted to see the Society opening up this enterprising new Gallery, and has told me to repeat her good wishes for its success in the future. As a connoisseur and collector Her Majesty was delighted to have this opportunity to see this enchanting collection of Turner water-colours, and sends her thanks to you for the informed tour of the pictures which she enjoyed in your company.

Yours sincerely,

William Heseltine

Ernest Greenwood, Esq.

The next morning a letter was delivered by post thanking me for the interesting morning Her Majesty had spent, and expressing her admiration for the enterprising work of the Society in establishing Bankside. This was also a great day for the RWS – it had been saved from extermination, or at least we thought it had, but there were 'growing pains' for years to come to combat complacency. The small staff were very much occupied in changing the character and reputation of an elite society into a forward looking organisation prepared to hold its own in a rapidly moving world as it approached the twenty-first century.

Writing these memoirs in 2005 leaves my optimism in grave doubt. Since my retirement much has happened to the Society since the senior members have withdrawn their active support or have died. Judy Dixy had been Director for eleven years before she moved on. Now the control of the Gallery to

BUCKINGHAM PALACE

19th March, 1983.

Dear Mr Greenwood,

Many thanks for your letter of March 17th which I shall lay before The Queen today. I am sure that Her Majesty will be very touched by your expressions of your gratitude on behalf of members of the Society who received their Diplomas signed in her own hand.

Yours sincerely

William Heseltine

Ernest Greenwood, Esq.

a non-member management has taken place, the councils of the RWS and RES will have reduced authority to make their voices heard at any future meetings. This drastic decision does seem retrogressive to me and, to my knowledge, is the most radical change that has ever taken place. But time alone will tell what will evolve from this action.

XII
VENICE AND AUSTRIA

We paid our first visit to Venice in 1952. We stayed in a house on the Zatare once used by Ruskin. Like all other visitors we were captivated by this enchanting city. Tourism had not yet reached its self-destructive zenith. You could still walk without difficulty along the narrow alleys and pause to look and enjoy the infinite variety of the city's architecture. The academia had so many treasures that we only knew from reproductions like, for example, 'The Tempest' by Giorgione which retains its strange mystery, a picture without a specified subject but one with an imaginative and poetic vision, and 'The Presentation of the Virgin', an early work by Titian that expresses so well the tentative steps of a little girl walking towards the unknown. The sixteenth century plague was a great blight causing the death of so many, not least amongst artists – Giorgione, Raphael, Massacio – just a few of the many who died young. Titian was an exception, like Michelangelo, who lived and worked into old age.

The intense romantic experience induced by Venice was enhanced on the evening when we joined a group of gondola all making their way to the centre of the Grand Canal. On

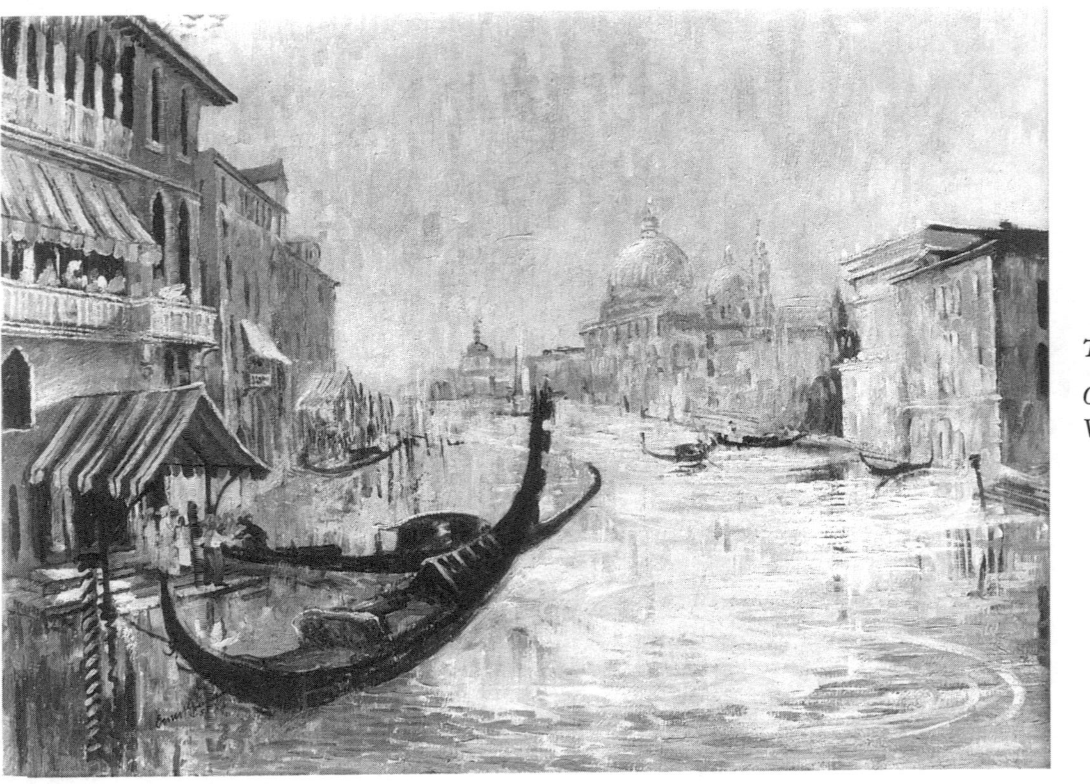

The Grand Canal

One of my paintings of Venice, 1954.

arriving they all linked up to form a water-born audience for a concert of excerpts from Italian Operas. In the warm, quiet atmosphere, under an inky-blue sky peppered with a multitude of stars, the only light came from lanterns and the twinkling light from Pallazi reflected in the slight movement of the water as though we had stars above and stars at our feet. Our visit included a canal journey down to the island of Torcelo, the original birth place of the city. It is now a quiet backwater dominated by its Lombardic-Romanesque Church and Campanile. I only had time to do a quick line drawing in one of my sketch books. The panoramic view of Venice on our return was wonderful. Of course, time was spent visiting the many churches, particularly because they still have, *in situ*, great paintings designed for a specific space under a special source of light. One of these visits took us to the island dominated by the Church of St. Giorgio Maggiore. This building contains a large assembly of works by Tintoretto which constitutes a whole collection of huge decorations that can be overwhelming because of their strength, size and power. Dorelia was with us and when turning into a corner into a side chapel exploded into 'not another Tintoretto'.

No one going to Venice could miss a visit to the glass factory on Murano. The skill and nonchalant manner in which molten glass was manipulated, twisted and spun in every conceivable shape or size was the result of years of experience, but not always with a satisfactory end product. We bought a small decanter in red with five small wine glasses, each decorated on the surface with a lace-like pattern which I think quite exquisite. This little set joins our collection of ten or more decanters which are a pleasurable reminder of our travels.

One morning, waiting for a vaporetta to take us down the Grand Canal, we found ourselves standing next to two ladies, a mother and daughter. We exchanged smiles in rather a crowded vessel, before disembarking for our own destinations. The next morning, on the same quayside, the same two ladies were waiting for canal transport. We were warmly greeted as old friends, as Fritzi and Erika became to us. They both said that English was the language they were studying and asked if we would mind if they joined us for the sake of exercising their vocabulary. So we spent the day with Fritzi and Erika, finding great pleasure in their company. Before we left them that day we exchanged addresses, hoping to meet again sometime. Well, sometime came and with it an invitation to visit them both in Vienna. We accepted the invitation gladly and meeting them again was a confirmation that we had many interests in common. They were both very good guides as we discovered when they took us to Schönbrunn, built for the Emperor Franz Joseph, together with the Gloriette. They provided a positive visual indication of what the Austrian Empire meant in the nineteenth century – its national pride, its wealth and aggrandisement of the capital.

The Ringstrasse, built on the foundations of the medieval curtain wall round Vienna was a beautifully harmonised architectural feature of an imaginative and sensitive type, a unique statement of self confidence. Unfortunately, a past City Council permitted the replacing of bomb-damaged sections with the use of the modern medium of steel and glass, as in Canterbury. I hope this kind of vandalism has been rectified by sensible replacement.

Wolfgansee is an impressive lake in the mountains in which we thought we might bathe, but the temperature was not much above freezing. This made a cancellation of this idea positive!

The nineteenth century steam train (now gone, I understand) was a wonderful relic of the past which, as far as I could see, was well worth preserving if only for its tourist value. I wonder if there is an enthusiastic preservation society busy putting it back again!

Back in Vienna another experience awaited us: Erika and Fritzi had booked a performance of Mozart's 'Don Juan' in the once Royal Theatre in Schönbrunn Palace. The theatre, newly decorated in deep red and gold, was gorgeous. Angels and cupids fluttered about from every balcony, symptomatic of the rococo ideal of the time. The engagement was an important social occasion for which formal dress was expected. I needed a jacket other than my black one so before we left for Austria I took myself off to Horne Bros and selected a dark blue/black needle cord (the tailor commented on my excellent choice) and we proceeded with the ceremony of taking measurements. In those far distant times Horne Bros of Piccadilly were very high-class tailors in equally first class premises. When walking into this establishment you were received with the utmost courtesy, which gave me the feeling that if I tripped up I would have disappeared into the pile of thick carpet. So I was in due course, without hurry, summoned to a first fitting of the garment in its temporarily stitched-up state. The tailor then proceeded to tear the jacket to pieces having liberally drawn with chalk a number of signs exclusive to tailors. In a week or ten days another card arrived announcing a time and date for another fitting. This time the object looked more like a jacket but then certain parts were torn apart again and I began to wonder for what year this garment was destined! However, my third fitting was the final one. I was helped into a piece of clothing never to be repeated. Some time afterwards a bill arrived for the grand total of five pounds (old money of course). I loved that jacket and wore it many times, over many years, following its baptism in Vienna. I had it in my wardrobe until quite recently and miss it now.

The Spanish Riding School in Vienna was something else to remember. Who could ever fail to retain the image of the two, the horse and the rider, in unison? I have always admired the beauty and the elegance of the horse, as have so many nations down the years. The Minoans in their little bronze stylised horses expressed one concept of an animal so many generations and nations have admired. But no people have ever held the horse in the esteem in which the Greeks did in the classical period. They set a standard in sculpture which has been the norm from Hellenistic, into Roman, Renaissance and modern times. As you would expect, the horses in the Spanish Riding School were groomed to enhance their beauty which was matched by the elegance of the mount. The dressage performance was just as impressive and one came away satisfied in every sense.

Our next trip was to a glacier which was on a gentle slope, making careful walking possible. The four of us started out to reach a walkers' hut some distance away. We walked and walked but as we proceeded the hut got further away! We gave up in the end, sat down and had a welcome lunch. In a sketch I have recorded a diminutive Erika under an equally diminutive tree, seen considering the prospect of the 'never, never' hut!

One of our trips was to a market where hot wurst were being sold. Fritzi thought we should try one. We sat at a table on a gravelled area while Erika went off to purchase one for each of us. Ours were firmly speared on a stick to make consumption easy but Erika's was not. It fell off and rolled under the table; she was furious when she saw the very alert pigeons swoop down and carry off her sausage. A short rail journey took us to another famous eating house, the building of which once formed part of a monastic foundation. Here, in 'Thalem', we sampled the speciality which was roast chicken – a serving consisted of a whole bird but they must have been small ones! I understand these medieval remnants of the monastery have been beautifully restored.

Uncle Leo Messenger was Eileen's only relative beyond her immediate family. He was a bachelor, a numismaticist, who I found interesting to study when I painted his portrait. Although I never saw his collection of coins I understand it was of considerable value and included a few the British Museum did not have. He had two silver vesta boxes found in a piece of his clothing that came to me when he died. They created an interest in this particular type of craftsmanship which became the nucleus of my collection of one hundred which I have passed on to Ian with my gold watch and chain. But the largest known collection of anything was the amassed number of cigarette cards of which my friend Edward Wharton-Tigar had over one million, all catalogued. This, the largest in the world, is recorded in the Guinness Book of Records. Edward started collecting as a small boy and has left the results of his early enthusiasm to the British Museum. Before the war Leo had an Austrian penfriend, a solicitor in Graz. After the war, Herr Schnieder wrote to Leo suggesting they might continue the friendship. Unfortunately, Leo had died and the letters were going to his brother, Eileen's father. He most categorically stated his lack of interest in the idea and handed the correspondence to us. We jumped at the idea and promptly wrote, stating our pleasure at the suggestion. And so our first foreign journey was to Austria to meet Herr Schnieder and his family. He met us on arrival, standing on the platform, holding a small bunch of flowers of welcome which was matched by his hospitality. During our short visit, his daughter married Ralph, a man with whom we got on very well. The daughter we were never sure of, she struck us as being flighty and superficial which was all too right. The marriage did not last long but long enough for Dorelia to act as one of the bridesmaids. Being British and therefore very practical our present to swell the pile of gifts was a pair of bath towels! Our first experience of travelling abroad was very instructive about people and their behaviour. Herr Schnieder had a vineyard and employed a man and his wife to run the business who had a little boy, Peter. We were taken up to the vineyard to be introduced and to inspect the property of which our host was very proud. What struck us forcibly was the relationship between the employer and the employee. The employee was looked upon as a peasant and treated as such. An attitude repeated some years later when we had an Austrian friend staying with us. We took her to a nearby village and standing on the green where cricket was played she looked around and said, 'And where are the peasants?' I replied, 'Oh! They all died with Wat Tyler!' We must have stayed in the vineyard house for a few days because Peter and Dorelia got on so well with Dorelia learning to speak a little German in a very short time.

So we left the vineyard and returned to Graz for a day or two before setting out for Kapfenberg where Schnieder had business to do. When crossing the bridge near the village of Peggou we stopped with the sole purpose of viewing the half submerged trucks lying in the river that were remnants of a war time incident. At the village our host insisted on stopping for breakfast. He ordered an omelette and while waiting for its arrival said, 'My omelette will have six eggs in it', then. 'The worst thing about the war here was nothing good to eat', followed by, 'You're a long time in the dark'. With this sinister remark he attacked his omelette like the greedy man he was judging by his size and how he ate heartily several times a day – food was very important to him. Our day's journey ended, I recall, in Kapfenberg, which was at that time in the Russian sector, where we were due to spend the night. But we were quite unprepared, having left Graz at the crack of dawn we had nothing except the clothing we were wearing. There was nothing much to buy in the town. We did manage to purchase a tooth brush and face flannel which constituted our overnight, minimal luggage. In the morning we were picked up and made the journey back to Graz without any further incidents.

Our third adventure, accompanied by the newly weds, was to Bad Ischl, notorious for its hot mud baths. There were wooden buildings constructed with heavy timbers that had a DIY look and in fact were not good examples of DIY anyway. The cubicles of wood linked one another by roughly-made doors which did not exclude the strong draughts, especially when left unclosed by the male attendant who would pass to and fro in order to keep the mud warm by some means or another. He obviously enjoyed to the full the presence of all the ladies, anxious to maintain their complexions by patronising his establishment. The cleansing and dressing was equally primitive, but all this will by now have disappeared to be replaced by plastic and modern hygiene equipment.

XIII
JOAN

DURING OUR TWENTY-FIVE YEARS in Bridge Cottage we employed a number of women to work in the house and to take an interest in our lives. The last and most loyal was Doris Goodwin and her husband, Ted. After our move Doris remained in our employment for a short time to help us combat a few major tasks in a house very much in need of tlc. Doris was wonderful in many respects. When coming to us from Otford she had quite a long walk to the station. I picked her up from Maidstone and drove her to Brushings. Her visits were a great help to us.

Two of the most urgent jobs on the house were the kitchen floor and back porch. The kitchen retained its original red-brick floor but because generations of hob-nailed boots on busy legs had walked to and fro, from the back floor to the pump in the far corner of the kitchen, some of the bricks on this route had deep holes in them. It was this area we tried to clean. A much greater hazard was the porch because the three steps down were short in the going and much too steep in the risers – it was on these we both had nasty falls. The roof over these steps was equally primitive, consisting of a piece of corrugated iron bent to form a pitch supported on two poles. After Doris left, as we knew she would, her husband Bert agreed to work with me on the porch problem. As he worked for a building company, Bert was happy to work on a task such as this one from start to finish so we designed a porch with a toilet on the right and on the left, space for an oak seat. Bert found a window for the toilet and made the door before he retired. It was some years later that we heard the sad news that Doris had had Alzheimer's and had died. We had a letter from Bert's daughter that her father was quite old and fragile and was unlikely to pay us the long promised visit and so out of our lives passed two faithful friends. For a short time, May, from the village worked at Brushings, followed by Mary who suffered from a complete lack of interest in anything. She managed to break two antique plates from a set of twelve which the family had treasured for about a hundred years.

This chapter is entitled 'Joan' because of the length of time she has devoted to us, a period that covers over thirty years of our lives. Joan told me that a neighbour of hers said she heard someone in Broad Street wanted help two days a week and on this scrap of information Joan met Meem in Maidstone and asked her if she was the person needing help in the house. That is how it all began in 1970. When I first met Joan she was the mother of five children living at Big Allington, in Anglo Saxon Elnorthington. Joan used to walk the mile or so from Big Allington to us when Susan, her baby girl, was in a pram. Later on she used a cycle. Walt, her husband, was working for Len Wright and continues to work for Dudley, his son. Len Wright was a countryman at heart but deficient (like so many farmers) in the appreciated of medieval buildings on his large estate. A barn at Big Allington, disused and derelict, was allowed to collapse. It was a curved corner timber from this barn that Len

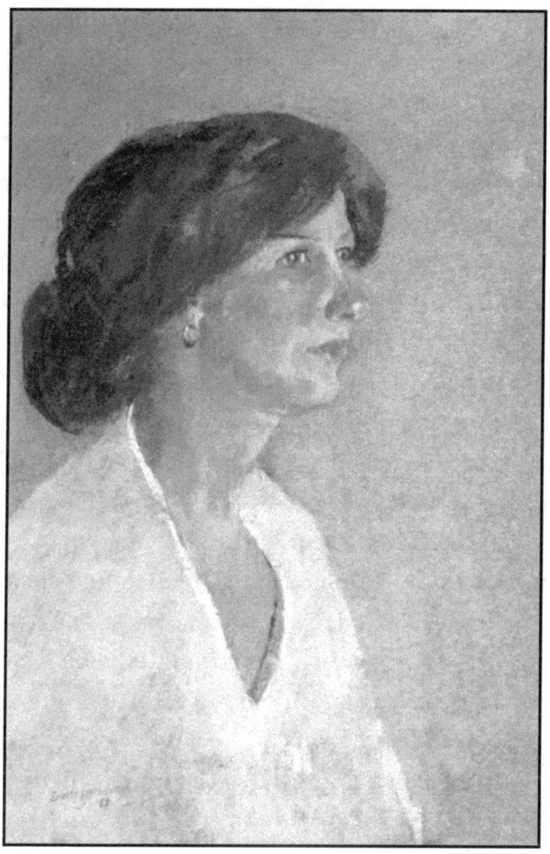

My portrait of Joan

Wright let me have to replace one on the left hand corner of 'Brushings' which we found missing when Gordon and I removed the hanging tiles which were disfiguring the front elevation. Joan told me it had been the home of a barn owl which all the farm workers knew about, which was found dead after the collapse, to everyone's sorrow. No barn owl has been seen in the area of Broad Street or Allington since, and probably never will as the number of habitats have gone. When we moved to Broad Street there were three large barns that have now all gone.

In the 1970s and '80s we did a considerable amount of entertaining in which Joan assisted with all the background work before the guests arrived and after they had gone. As the years went by, Joan gradually became more integrated into the family, more so after helping Dorelia at The Ringlestone for a short time. Being a country girl she had a keen interest in plants and wildlife. She was pleased to increase her time with us to work in the garden, especially as the site developed.

During our forty-three years in Broad Street fundamental changes took place, particularly noticeable after Len Wright died. He kept a large herd of cattle which when they moved from one pasture to another, passed the house. It was a large herd, led by the bull, with Bob Law, the foreman, and Tom Eldrett in charge. They, and Charlie, a countryman born and bred, all lived in the hamlet giving the genuine character of country life which I loved, even when, during one of our parties, one of Len Wright's sows got through the hedge into our garden. I had the pleasure of helping her back into the field with a whack on the rear.

Walt bred pheasants in the woods below the house and was furious when a motorist tried to run one down. These birds frequently came into the garden on their clumsy, fluttering flight, on food-hunting expeditions that we encouraged.

Then Joan met Dick, or Dick met Joan, I am not sure how – I think it may have been giving Joan a lift to Hollingbourne on several occasions. Anyway, the inevitable happened and Dick offered Joan the prospect of a new and better life which she accepted. And so Joan left Big Allington to marry Dick, a self-employed builder, a very good craftsman who was well-informed on many things. This turn of events put us in a difficult situation because Walt had done a number of jobs for us. We quite liked him for what he was, a simple countryman.

During the domestic and emotional upheaval which ensued, Walt came to us for help over the break up of his home. We did what we could in as sympathetic a way as we knew how, but we were quite unable to alter the decisions of others. So Walt left us an unhappy man. I think he now lives in a cottage on Dudley's estate with an unmarried daughter with a child.

Meem and I were witnesses at Joan and Dick's marriage. They now live in Marsham Street, Maidstone, having done so for over twenty-four years. Both Joan and Dick are fond of all members of her innumerable daughters, sons-in-law, grandchildren and great-grandchildren for good measure! Joan keeps in touch with them all. Christmas and birthdays must make quite an impression of the purse! Since moving to Lakeside, Joan has travelled from Marsham Street to us by car. She is as faithful as ever, coming to Lakeside three times a week to assist two elderly people who are finding help increasingly necessary. The maintenance of domestic efficiency gradually becomes more difficult with the decline of physical energy. The many common tasks which were once done automatically and then forgotten are now major problems which demand an inordinate amount of time and thought. It is all these jobs, which were once trivialities, which now demand younger hands in order to retain acceptable standards which Joan recognises and understands so well. In this, she is irreplaceable. Dick also worked at Brushings for many years as will be seen later on, there was a lot to do!

Joan has had her life considerably enlarged since her marriage to Dick. Their interests have fluctuated from fishing, camping, cycling and walking, but the last two have dominated, at least for Dick, who enjoys being a member of a racing club. They also take walking holidays together with a group who have many similar interests. The continuation of this happy relationship now hangs in the balance as Joan and Dick, understandably, are looking for a property to buy in which to settle permanently on retirement.

XIV

BRUSHINGS FARMHOUSE AND BROAD STREET

IT WAS IN THE TWENTY-FIFTH YEAR of our tenancy at Bridge Cottage that we begun to think seriously about buying a place of our own. The desire to own an ancient house in the countryside like my Aunt's house in Little Hawksley where I spent my childhood holidays remained with me. I suppose this need was part of the predilection I had towards the historical-romantic in music and literature. The former was established when I was very young through the piano playing of an Aunt whose performances had the power to awaken such emotions in me when aged twelve to thirteen. Subconsciously, having lived so long in Bridge Cottage I was anxious, with Meem, to find the right place which meant a long search. We were both working, I was in London and Meem was in Kent, so these factors restricted the perimeter of our search. We motored to every possible advertised property that was in any way approaching our requirements. One weekend we came to Maidstone and walking down the High Street paused to look in the window of Hamiltons Estate Agent. In the window was a photograph of a flint chimney stack surrounded in daffodils. Thinking this might be a good omen we entered and obtained a viewing appointment. The house had suffered quite long periods of neglect and was in urgent need of tlc inside and out, but the environment was wonderful.

Accompanied by the owner we looked over the house, ducking under a huge tie beam when going underneath into the bathroom I looked back at Meem and said, 'This is it!' So we paid the deposit of two thousand pounds but it bounced! We did not have this sum of money, so I began another search for someone to lend me two thousand. It was suggested by a person, I can no longer remember who, that I might try a certain bank in Camberwell, so to this bank I went, announced my identity and was shown into the Managers Office. On being seated he said how pleased he was to see an officer from the LCC as he was worried about his daughter who was a student at Camberwell School of Art. She had made a boyfriend with whom he did not approve and could I help? I explained my position as well as he would let me before asking the question I had come to ask. All I got was a suggestion that I should go down to New Cross, to a friend of his managing a bank there. I went with not much hope, a sentiment that was justified, because I got no help from him either by which time I was feeling a bit glum. So, the next day I called on the solicitor handling the sale who was very helpful. I recall to mind so well the Dickensian office, his large leather bound chair, his avuncular smile of confidence as he recommended I try the manager of the bank with whom we did our financial business. But I said, 'I have tried there without success'. 'Oh well', he said 'Call again'. So off I went to Sevenoaks and found a very sympathetic ear and got my two thousand pound loan. Had Douglas Gulland phoned on my behalf? I do not know, but I have my suspicions. The result of this anxious time (I was so afraid the house would be sold) was so stressful for me – I lost two stone in weight. But we succeeded and became the owners of Brushings Farm House, the great event in our lives.

The KCC had already made the arrangement to deduct monthly from Eileen's salary the loan necessary to cover the gap in the purchase price. This is where the work began. I have already mentioned the kitchen floor and back porch which were top priorities. Before we could tackle the brick floor an ugly, small coke boiler had to be removed. The second thing was the replacement of the Aga, the existing one had been so badly used that it was now useless. This was an unexpected expense but we managed. The brick floor was started soon afterwards. The name of the workman who did the kitchen tiled floor is now forgotten but it was a quick job once the materials had been delivered. The bricks were carefully stacked and all reused later on. These two operations transformed the room, without in any way being detrimental, into a splendid kitchen.

When we bought Brushings Farm House the two rooms forming dining and sitting areas were separated by lath and plaster between the structural timbers. This included a door into the areas itself and one at the bottom of the staircase. We decided to remove the doors into the sitting room and stairs. But I must go back a year or two to introduce Gordon, who I think was brother-in-law to the workman who tiled the kitchen floor. Gordon had already built the retaining wall and installed the iron panels to the back of the garage. He was a first class craftsman and we got on well. We took off the cheap braced and ledged doors and cut away the plaster work with a strong knife in large squares for easy removal – a dirty, dust job. This left a hole in the flooring through which we could see straight into the cellar, something we should have anticipated. But what a transformation this work made to the area; it was greater than we thought it would be and so much lighter. In one go we had doubled the living space.

The stairs were quite wide, but rather dark, so we asked Gordon to make a window frame to match the remaining medieval examples of which we had a number; one in our bedroom, the bathroom and the long closet between the second and third bedrooms. This wind-eye retained its original glazing bars although there was no evidence that glass had ever been used. Gordon used a piece of oak that came from the demolished barn. He made a perfect replica which was lovely to look at and feel. The next job was on the back stairs, like the two down stairs, the back landing was boxed in to conserve heat but the installation of central heating made these partitions unnecessary. At the top of the back stairs a door had been installed to link with the wall at right angles to it. I removed the door first and found it fitted perfectly into the door frame of the long closet because the latch had been left in place. When I demolished the wall shuttering in the landing space I found, under a thin layer of plaster, a wall made of near rubbish. It was in this area that Gordon worked using four of the oak timbers I had saved. These formed a frame for the iron decorative panels which replaced the wall.

Before we started work on the front elevation, the bathroom was next for a complete overhaul. The bathroom had glazed floor to ceiling cupboards. It also housed the hot water heater. Immediately next to this unit was a door opening on to the back landing and studio stairs. This under stairs area provided enough space into which an airing cupboard could be made and a water heater fitted. This was a major move. It left an area where the hand basin could be removed from its position next to the bath into a specially designed unit with cupboards underneath. It transformed the look of this part of the house particularly as it had a direct link with the back landing.

The gloomy appearance of the front elevation was made by dark brown tiles. When we began to remove them we found an enormous mess made by the generations of house sparrows pecking holes in the plaster. As work proceeded we could see and estimate the damage done. We also uncovered a small square window which I mentioned when explaining the long closet. Having been protected from the weather it was perfectly preserved. As we moved along, conservation went on at the same time to timbers and panels. On reaching the last section on the right we found one curved beam supporting the corner which had been removed in order to make the new windows symmetrically arranged along the front. Now, during my moving walks with our dog I noticed that there was, in the collapsed barn, just what I wanted. Len Wright willingly gave it to me and the next weekend I transported it back to Brushings. When the work was finished and all plastered areas were painted white the house sparkled.

Gordon eventually worked longer than he might have done because the owner of the house in which he and his wife Ciss lived was anxious to sell the property. They needed six hundred pounds urgently and asked if we could lend them the money if he worked it off in labour. So Gordon continued to work on our improvements in which the front elevation was perhaps the most important job of all. The buildings outside the kitchen window were in a deplorable condition. On two brick piers there was a huge rectangular storage tank. Judging by the thick layer of sludge it had not been used for many years. This had to be removed which was no easy task but we managed. The council charged seven pounds to take it away.

The slopes of the garden were attractive enough but necessitated building twenty four steps from the front gate to the back porch. I did this work myself and this is where some of the kitchen bricks were used. In order to simulate paving slabs I used a template, turning it around to give variety. This job took me weeks – I was always mixing concrete, but it lasted forty years and I imagine is being used now. The fall of the land made retaining walls essential. Over the years we created a walled garden, the last part being the boundary between us and the farm which was only done after the sale of the property to Batchelor. This meant more steps! The new porch projected beyond the line of the house, making a wide path, six foot six inches, leading up to the small gate in the wall. This meant six more steps which used most of the kitchen floor bricks, but the final result had a generous look that we enjoyed. The walled garden was used for growing vegetable which we protected with netting on metal poles. During one winter we had a freak fall of snow which completely demolished the lot. So, after the mess had been cleared up we changed our minds and decided to have a walled herb garden, but we still needed a flat area that we did not have. The fall across the plot was about four foot which I said I would level while Meem designed the herb garden, so this is what we did. Now I had several tons of soil to shift and I knew I would only do this slowly, systematically, so I stuck to the ten barrow loads a day method. As the days went by I could see no difference whatsoever so I dug a number of holes, driving pegs in, giving the necessary height from which to work. I used a board and spirit level placed on these pegs to check the levels. After a month or so I began to see some advance was being made. A neighbour who had a horse and sheep wanted somewhere to dump the stable sweepings. I gave him the answer then all at once I saw the change and success. By this time Meem had completed a design on graph paper ready for our builder from which to work. The following spring we saw the fruits of our labour.

The new landowner wrote demanding that we removed our cess pit onto our own land. This was quite an expense that we did not expect, but not a surprise considering the nature of the man. Several years on when we bought the field it would have been on our land anyway. Batchelor's greed caused his bankruptcy.

Two big jobs remained to be done. The first was to extend the garage by taking the roof over to our boundary which gave security for the fuel tank. A door in the bricked contiguous wall provided space for a door, an ideal garage for the mower. As Meem's retirement from the college approached I knew she would need a major interest to take its place and somewhere to work. A lean to building lent itself to refurbishment perfectly, being so close to the back porch, but it did require a lot of work to be done. This building had been the well house and coke store. It was very dirty but it had potential. Following the fall of the land the building was in two parts on different levels. The lower part had been a hen house with a door giving direct access to the garden. The first thing was to make one of the two parts and convert them into a studio for Meem's exclusive use. I started work on the hen house. I removed the door and bricked up the opening with the bricks from the garden. The site was, at some time, lived in by a man who made a poor living collecting other people's rubbish judging by what I found or dug up. I next put in joists to raise the floor level almost to that of the main building and looked down the flimsy partition. We now had one building, not two. The central heating unit in the well house area was taking up too much space so, in order to gain this space, I extended the front by building a second wall about six foot high from the original one, giving us about thirty-six square feet. My bricklaying was not up to Winston Churchill's but mine is standing after forty years! The original outer door I re-hung and so completed an L-shape studio which Meem used for nearly thirty years.

The well was dry; the water table had fallen owing to pumping stations being installed on, or near the Pilgrim's Way. We were curious to know whether it would contain anything of historic interest so we had the well excavated. The two men doing the job went down thirty foot lower than the flint and brick sides but nothing was found apart from the remains of the uniform of a Captain in the New Zealand Engineers. So the well was sealed, cemented over, which produced a slight step up from the original floor. This was all very fine if the corrugated iron roof had not leaked, so this was removed and replaced with slates and two skylights. Slate was chosen because the pitch was too slight for tiles. In time, this made a good studio once the walls were covered with wall-board and painted white.

The garden wall on the coming out of the house was partly broken down and had formed a convenient passage for the disposal of household rubbish on the land beyond, which included clinkers from the boiler and lots of them. Two pear trees suffering form a lack of nutrients had almost given up the struggle. What shall we do with this unused area? Clear the rubbish first, as far this was feasible. The archway and brick wall were built so we decided to make a water garden, but I had to repair the broken down part of the wall first and also lay water pipes under the paving to take rain water from the roof to the third pond. The slope of the land was a help when making the ponds. It enabled us to have three ponds with water flowing from upper to lower. The work took quite a long time, it included a fountain in a circular and larger pool and a pump to take water to the top through a rocky outlet. This provided a very pleasant sound of falling water. A year or two before the rapid decline of the frog population we had the top pond almost full of these mating creatures making a croaking cacophony. We had seen no frogs in the garden up to the time we left.

In the first few pages of these memoirs I indicated that the nature of my ambition was to live in a medieval house in rural surroundings. Brushings Farm House fulfilled this perfectly.

When moving into Broad Street I was settling into a small community, the centre of a large estate owned by Leonard Wright who worked the land with his son Dudley and the foreman Bob Law with Tom Eldrett and casual labour. In one of the two Pilgrim's Cottages lived Charlie and his wife. Charlie had lived and worked on a farm all his life. As a young man he lived in Leeds and on Saturdays he and his palls walked into Maidstone and back as transport was almost non-existent. As I said about my boyhood, if you did not walk you stayed where you were. Now, children do not even walk to the bus stop. This observation emphasises one of the fundamental changes that have taken place since the end of the Second World War, changes not always for the good.

I have wondered why the passing of Len Wright's great herd of cattle, with the massive bull in attendance, always gave me such pleasure. The drovers would always have a pleasant word as the animals wandered leisurely by.

The stable wall formed a part of our boundary, but alas, there were no horses. At right angles to the land and a little further into the field stood a magnificent Tythe barn in which Len housed his pigs. He seemed unconcerned that these animals were doing serious damage to the building. A few years later Len discontinued breeding pigs so the barn stood empty and neglected. One morning we were alarmed to see a casual worker stripping off all the tiles from the roof and much more, so when were sae tractors demolishing such a splendid example of farm architecture we were horrified. Conservations concern came too late to save this gem. Behind the house, some mile or two away, the woods covered a hill which formed a welcome barrier to the railway and motorway. It was in these woods that Walt, Joan's first husband, working for Len, bred game birds. Over this he took a pride and was furious when a motorist tried to run one down.

At the end of Broad Street lived the Hortons, in what had been Broad Street Farm. They moved into the hamlet a few weeks following us. Peter Horton kept a milking cow and hens, just another small addition to our country life. Across the land, right opposite the Hortons lived Tom Eldrett, in Cedar Bungalow – a tiny wooden building that Tom found adequate for his needs. His wife must have died soon after we moved in to Brushings because we only knew Tom as one of Len Wright's employees. On his retirement he worked for Beryl and Peter – a man who was exclusively devoted to Beryl, for whom he did everything. When Beryl died Tom had little incentive to live a lonely, purposeless existence in his minute bungalow. He died after a short illness in hospital shortly after Beryl. Tom's bungalow is now no more. It was demolished to make way for a small, well-designed house in sympathetic materials which will soon become part of the body of the hamlet. Tom's little house is probably now only preserved in a painting of mine, but I am unaware of its whereabouts.

Our English Setter demanded exercise, so we took it together, each morning, what-ever the weather. I always carried a sketch book with me in which I made notes, or frequently more complicated statements for future use. Each morning, of course, was quite different from the preceding one; such a contrast to the mornings in Arizona which were lovely but unchanging.

Our walks were not always long ones but were exploratory; I found many things to record and remember that were not always pleasant. One morning, on approaching the style into the meadow overlooking Broad Street I saw that a lorry load of rubbish had been left to completely disfigure the copse through which I was about to walk. A few weeks after this mess had been cleared, on the same spot I found a burnt out car, on another, a pile of broken glass. The penalties for this pollution of our countryside should be severe. Broad Street from the meadow above Hillside House I found captivating under all weather conditions. The farm buildings and houses, many of them old ones, seemed to grow out of the soil to become a permanent part of the landscape as they must have looked for years past.

One weekend we were busy in the kitchen when an old, bright green van, drew up outside the front gates and two or three people got out and gave the house a long stare before coming in. Very apologetically they announced themselves as Australians who had come to England in order to find the house where their father had been billeted during his army service in the war. He had described the house in detail. They were delighted to have identified the house and asked, 'May we take some pictures?' They were charming and quite happy to have photographs to take back home.

Another interested occurrence took place in 1979 before the gale destroyed the row of lime trees which grew in the front hedge. This is the time to mention the great storm.

There were four, fine mature lime trees in the front hedge which the gale blew down. Fortunately the prevailing winds took them from the house and into the lane. Had it been in the opposite direction it would have done untold damage to the house and us too! Of course, this made the passage of anything past the garden impossible for several hours while all the neighbours with chainsaws got to work on the blockage. The bowls of these trees were enormous when wrenched from the soil. All we could do was to light a fire inside the stump and so burn them away. It took weeks. I remember the advent of our other visitors so well because they could only see the house through a gap between the trees, but they too were curious and indicated at the gate that they would like to come in, which they did. Two quite old ladies with white hair and Edwardian mourners introduced themselves as sisters who had been born in the house when it was a real farmhouse. We heard from them again when they sent us some very old sepia photographs of the house surrounded with chickens running about in a very rough garden area. There was also an outside staircase to the stables which had gone before we arrived. These pictures of the past gave us a glimpse into the life of Broad Street as it was just after the First World War ended.

I found the cellar one of the most intriguing parts of the house as it contained a very large oak beam which supported the dining and sitting rooms above. It really was a very large timber which must have been taken from an old, mature tree. Although I have no means of knowing its age it must have been one hundred and fifty years old when felled. The house was built about five hundred years ago, making that essential support about six hundred and fifty years old. The other associated feature was the cloam oven of which the original cover is still in place. The earth oven was dismantled when the cellar steps were made, replacing the first ones which were sited in the sitting room cupboard – our bar! In the land opposite the flint chimney there are remnants of foundations of a small building that might have been a bakery or brew house. The coins we found on this patch suggest that trade of some sort was done.

It was about 1985 or earlier that we had a surprise in receiving a letter from Pauline, Roy and Simon Taylor who owned an antique book shop. This lead to an interesting correspondence and eventually a visit to Brushings in which we learned a great deal about their book shop and their love of rural France. Pauline had obtained news of us though a contact she had made with my sister Rose in the early '80s which continued with Connie on the death of Rose.

We spent most of our travels in France and the ancient world of Greece and Rome. We thought we should explore the countries further north so we booked a cruise on the *Black Prince*, the Fred Olsen line, scheduled to visit fjords and coastal towns, terminating at the cape. The ship left from Harwich which made the visit to Roy and Pauline a very pleasant way of being introduced to their home, where we spent the night with them before sailing the next morning. Unfortunately, there was no time to visit the shop, which we should have loved to have done. We are most unlikely to see it now.

Pauline and Simon's other great interest is in the history of the family. They have spent many hours in Her Majesty's Stationery Office in research and have traced our roots back to the seventeenth century, confirming that the families lived mainly in or near Lambeth Palace, but not in it! These unknown relatives would seem to be our forebears who were at the beginning of the line. When Roy died he left the shop in the very capable hands of Simon and Pauline. They visit houses where libraries are being sold on the death of their owners, the result producing a very specialised collection of great books. Apart from our shared interest in books, Simon and Pauline are enthusiastic Francophiles, going to France each year on their bicycles with the only purpose of visiting villages and small towns well away from the tourist routes. We receive the cards they send annually with interest, particularly as they often include places with which we are familiar. The most recent letter came this Christmas with most disturbing information about the occupants of premises next door to the shop. In January a young woman assaulted Pauline because she was refused entry into the shop. Pauline has had to prosecute a young man who threatened arson against the shop because she refused to allow him to park on her car park. The police were involved in both cases and were most supportive. This was not all; a young woman was locked out from entering the premises next door and was so drunk that she did not know where she was going. Antisocial behaviour is usually associated with teenagers but with adults it is deplorable. Years ago this could never have happened – 'spare the rod and spoil the child'.

I am compelled to speak of one more criminal act that caused the death of an old lady friend of mine. Shortly after her husband's funeral, Agnes moved into a flat. It was broken into and she was knocked about and robbed. She died from her injuries. Thinking of the evils and felonious manifestations of past and present violence in society is not a subject to dwell on. There are still so many things on our earth uncontaminated by man to enrich and inspire. Since my immobility places me in a position in my chair to watch the dawn, I have been free enough to ponder on this remarkable phenomenon which we take for granted. Weather conditions and the seasons give the dawn its great diversity, providing a subject for poets, painters and philosophers.

Einstein's theory of relativity is demonstrated when considering the earth revolving on its tilted axis in relation to the movement of the universe travelling in infinite space. Infinity is an incomprehensible conception for me. It many ways it is difficult to relate the idea of relativity when there seems to be no means of comparison between some contemporary works. The world wide expansion of modern art, the thinking and writing which has supported this fundamental change (which began in twentieth-century Europe, spread into America and has now taken root in Japan) has still left a number of artists unconvinced. For example, amongst a collection of works decorating certain areas in Tucson University there are two which demonstrate the existing dichotomy between practitioners. One of these was a huge metal cube with counter change squares of about twelve inches painted in yellow and black. The second was a life-sized sculpture of an Indian woman; the form was simple but significant – her feet, which came just below eye level were most beautifully modelled, rather in the manner of an Egyptian sculpture. The whole figure had a dignity, a powerful empathy, even a suggestion of the many problems, social and aesthetic, which were the concern of the artist when creating this sculpture. The work of Donatello and painting by Masaccio had influenced, subconsciously, the thinking along traditional lines that had stimulated the creative energy of the artist in producing this sculpture. The painted cube said nothing because it had nothing to communicate.

I suppose for many people things have moved too fast. In the 1930s Sir William Rothenstein, the principal of the Royal College of Art, represented a tradition that emphasised the importance of draughtsmanship as being of paramount importance for excellence in any field. Today these values have gone, their place has been taken by the production of what is euphemistically called modern art which incorporates anything new, often inane or trivial. Providing it is big, like the Tucson cube, it will be tolerated and paid for.

XV
PAST AND PRESENT

FROM THE PRECEDING CHAPTERS some indication of what the building, garden and more distant environment of Brushings meant to me is evident. Brushings Farm House was much more to me than a physical reality, it was continually reminding me of time, but time for me was, to a large extent, filled with a poetic unreality. Nevertheless, this imaginative part of life had and gave power and energy to every day and encouraged reading in the need to know more. The building breathed; the house, the surrounding meadows and woods made my best painting possible, helped by the books amongst which I worked. This is when time stood still, when the painting was all that mattered, sometimes growing out of an ephemeral beginning, sometimes failing completely.

In these memoirs I have attempted to select from a very active life those events which had a profound influence on my development. The growing-up process had been over a long period. My education, which began in the twenties, was in a society that no longer exists that was controlled by ideas that are no longer valid. This profound change had been brought about by two factors; the wide distribution of wealth and the now, world-wide use, sometimes misuse, of electrical technology. The first stimulated the second; both have contributed towards the nation's decline, while bestowing benefits on many. My upbringing was my education in one sense; even moderately bad language was never heard. There was no insidious media to pollute the language of communication but it had been born in the wireless set and cat's whisker. From now on the drift into mediocrity began and continues. Education at home consisted of teaching the essentials of social behaviour governing good life. But there are indications from the decline in acceptable social standards and in the growth of juvenile crime of every sort that good example and leadership are not exerted on the young. Is this the responsibility of parenthood or the production of children being passed on to the many official organisations who are dealing with the results at great cost? The proliferation of the cartoon in television viewing is a substitute for the lack of more commendable material which becomes more difficult to find as additional channels are opened. Of course, there are also the advertisements which interrupt, every ten minutes or more, the few good programmes broadcast.

Education, in my experience, has suffered more by the biased and bigoted interference of politicians than is realised. Twenty five years in the education service controlled by political dogma were twenty five years almost wasted, as will be gathered by anyone reading these memoirs. My wife and I were pioneers at Chislehurst Technical High School for Girls, now gone. Eileen was a pioneer at Battersea College of Domestic Science, now gone. For me, fifteen years in the London Education service were totally unproductive and not enjoyable. This too is now gone.

The twelve one-man exhibitions of my paintings were not

without their problems either. Employment in Kent was very enjoyable though – working with John Haynes, the Education Officer, on another pioneering project proved to be of great value in promoting an appreciation of the arts (Charlemagne, an early tenth century Emperor of the Holy Roman Empire recognised the value of the arts in the education of his subjects), but a change in the county elections put into power a majority who, looking for a way of saving money, immediately axed the art project, the result of six years work and expenditure. The visual material acquired at great cost was disposed of, so nothing remains. Following the example of Charlemagne did not help Kent.

But I think the most appalling display of political bigotry happened in my last association with the county when I staged in the space now known as the art gallery, my last one-man exhibition. It happened to contain some of my more successful paintings of the North Downs and I was looking forward to the event especially as the Lord Lieutenant of Kent, Lord Pemberton, had agreed to open the exhibition. The arrangements of this exhibition were in the hands of the curator who was allegedly in charge of advertising, hanging and publicity. Very little happened and much less if I had not provided a detailed drawing of the hanging arrangement plus a list of those I wished to be notified about the private viewing. No publicity, not even to the local press and only a handful of the people on my mailing list ever received a card. This was proved when the unsold work was returned with several unopened packs of catalogues numbering many hundreds were offered to me! In fact, they were all destroyed. The catalogue issue was the last straw. All the relevant material was sent to the so-called curator some weeks ahead. Time went by and nothing happened until, a day or two before the posting date, I received a proof of the catalogue printed in black, resembling a mourning card, plus the instruction that because the person who was to have opened the exhibition had been the Governor of the Bank of England and therefore a Conservative, he in no way would be allowed to open the exhibition and would I write and tell him so!

This is where my friend, Felicity Simpson, a member of the Council was wonderful. She offered and wrote a letter to Lord Pemberton explaining the situation in County Hall and helped in the catalogue crisis. It was pouring with rain when she picked me up and drove me to Springfield where we met and discussed the matter with a helpful person concerned with printing. The catalogues were delivered in time but it was not a good beginning to an event which was a disaster. However, our great friend Dan Leach (the collector of paintings and ceramics) did come over from Arizona in order to buy Eileen's favourite painting! Dan's visit to Maidstone just to see the show was just one of the many friends we had the pleasure of meeting that afternoon. Two of the visitors were old friends I was to see for the last time.

We knew a move from Brushings was inevitable. We saw it coming but with trepidation and anxiety. There was so much to lose and what would, or could take its place? Nothing.

So Eileen and Dorelia made a number of exploratory visits to places in Kent which seemed possible – most were not! Before coming to Lakeside permanently we paid two visits; one of two weeks, a second of three, at the conclusion of which we decided to buy apartments at Lakeside. As a temporary measure we occupied No. 36 when negotiations began which continued for months as nothing would be done to the rooms until paid for. It was all the business of purchasing that took so much time and energy. All this time Brushings was being cleared in my absence. I had to stay at Lakeside because of my inability to walk. So clearing was done thoroughly, completely, including many things I would like to have retained, but they have all gone. We managed to bring with us to Lakeside a few of the most precious things: our dresser, grandfather clock, Grandma Messenger's nursing chair, our bedside units and the work table. With these and few other things we live in our new abode. We are doing our best to start another phase, make new friends and find a new rhythm by which to live a routine that will reduce daily work tasks that become more difficult from year to year.

This new rhythm had been given substantial assistance by our Weald-care staff. The women who come in the morning and evening are, for the most part, charming and competent. They attend to my medical needs and equipment, give me helpful advice when required and their friendly attitude is a support when problems arise which seem difficult to solve. This team are mostly women with families of their own and are therefore familiar with the daily requirements of health and hygiene. The Lakeside staff in the dining room serve us all very well. The menus follow a pattern which are repeated but provide a sufficient variety and choice to make it a pleasure to use the restaurant.

Our problem of giving Oskar a morning and afternoon walk has been solved by a neighbour, Tony Walker, who is very pleased to walk with a dog for company and, as a consequence, has become very fond of him. In fact, Oskar has become quite a celebrity and is so pleased to be made a fuss of by every visitor. Perhaps the most difficult thing about residing at Lakeside is living with so many other disabled people. The fact that I happen to be one accentuates the absence of the vitality of younger company.

In these memoirs I have once or twice referred to the decline of the nation and some of my reasons for making such a statement. One reason for thinking as I do occurred recently. A certain Marcel Duchamp placed a urinal in an exhibition and declared it to be a work of art because he said so! But posterity decides what is or is not a work of art. The arrogance of the artist counts for little. Further, what do you judge a urinal with, other than with tens of thousands of identical urinals produced commercially? Duchamp should have submitted this for the Turner Prize! But there is still plenty to do, to look forward to each morning. Meem is back on her computer, and at present I am trying to make something of my memoirs, writing being a substitute for drawing and painting. There is also plenty to think about as intellectual critics make a mockery of past achievements in their support of the most fatuous and inane products of our own times.

The moral convictions and social behaviour in the life of a nation begin in the very young. We all learn by imitation, by copying others, usually from our parents in the first instance, but if this is lacking then the strongest and most attractive influence will not begin to educate. It is through the eyes, from television that this aspect of education takes place inside and outside of the home. Better would be the reading, collecting and care of books as they enlarge vocabulary and stimulate thought and imagination. They can also provide a spur to creative energy and give a basis from which to criticise and assess the value of things seen on television. They might question the emphasis given on every aspect of sex, on football, on jazz and ugly cartoons that were once the exclusive substance of a child's comic and are now being dished up for adult entertainment.

The twentieth century, like every preceding one, has experienced many changes in beliefs, standards and attitudes of the nation. The extent of these changes in Britain from suffragette to unisex has completely altered the treatment of men and women in their relationship with one another, a relationship which had governed mutual behaviour for many centuries. The social problems have, to a considerable extent, emerged from the disintegration of family unity. In too many cases parents have not made a lasting commitment to each other – the results are all too obvious; children left to themselves fall prey to leaders of antisocial groups.

The world wars have accelerated and seen the development of a complete distribution of every aspect of technology especially in the field of communication which has converted days and weeks into seconds for the transmission of information, not always good or relevant to national and international problems. We have been subjected to much verbiage about education, the charts, positions and degrees of performance (this morning – April 14th – government complains that children, not kids!, are still not being taught to read) that reveals the value or lack of it in such statistics and itself adds up to nothing helpful in encouraging children to become informed, intelligent and sensitive adults, in short, to become civilised. I am reminded of a book called *The Courtier* by Castiglione, a sixteenth century Tuscan, when he, writing on education says that 'good masters not only teach children their letters and skills but also polite manners and correct bearing in eating, drinking, speaking and walking'. We could do nothing better than add these virtues to the National Curriculum as it might help to reduce the tolerance to bad language in school and on film.

April 16th news was not good which only emphases the poor condition in which the nation presents itself to the world.

The loss of the production, at Longbridge, of Rover cars will only add to the enrichment of other manufacturers ready to fill the gap. The loss of Rolls Royce was bad enough, which should have alerted governments of a possible repetition, but no, we flounder on. Rather than halt national decline, the government seems intent on increasing it. We reduce the navy by nine ships; we reduce the army by disbanding regiments like the Black Watch. Will it be the RAF next? All these reductions in the armed forces will add a few thousand more to those on unemployment benefits. And how long will the term UK be relevant? The Second World War was not won by the English, the Welsh, Scots, or Irish alone, but by a unified force of representatives from the inhabitants of the British Isles. If this unity should be broken, as some short-sighted politicians are aiming at, then we each automatically become weaker. It could also damage unity in the Commonwealth and finally, of course, our one greatest asset we singularly gain by having a head of state who is not a politician, the Queen – long may the monarchy last! But the government had continued the trend of its policy from the start by abolishing the Royal Tournament. This was the only entertainment contributing towards our unity as a United Kingdom that on some feeble pretext of expense the chancellor could not justify, but he could justify spending millions or billions on a futile war in which they searched for a non-existent bomb and to which there is no foreseeable termination.

And so our life here continues. We deal with problems personal and collectively as best we can. Although I am aware there are many people with disabilities worse than mine, being unable to walk imposes restriction and a dependence on others, especially Meem who has an arthritic problem of her own to deal with. Looking back over eighty years I seem to have travelled a long way, but not alone. Eileen has travelled with me a similar distance since we met on the National Gallery steps and then visited the Westminster Abbey Cloisters which cemented our relationship and led to the brief wedding ceremony in a Registry office in 1939. Since those early days a great deal has taken place from the time of our marriage, precipitated by the war, to the present in Hothfield. Two unexpected and equally unpleasant experiences took place when I was swept off to the William Harvey Hospital where I spent twelve days. My second absence from No. 35 Lakeside was to give Meem a rest from taking care of my needs so I spent three weeks in a respite unit, but I will not linger over these two breaks in our lives at Lakeside as they were not happy ones.

As with most of us at this stage, we drop in to a low gear, but as I am blessed with wonderful eyesight I can read. I do not mean the daily newspapers, we have not bothered with one for over sixty years; I am referring to books. Literature stimulates thinking which in turn enables assessments to be made, especially over a long period of time. Our lives have not lacked difficulties as each new challenge, in professional terms, has always demanded more from us that we thought at the outset we could manage. But each new demand has enriched our lives and given us a broad, thoughtful attitude towards humanity. Some thoughts have not been entirely optimistic about the future as we drift further and further away from standards I thought, as a child, were permanent. But like the days of the 'Haywain', they too have gone for a new century; it has gone for what we hope will be a *Brave New World*.